DECADES

Alice Cooper

in the 1980s

Chris Sutton

sonicbondpublishing.com

Sonicbond Publishing Limited
www.sonicbondpublishing.co.uk
Email: info@sonicbondpublishing.co.uk

First Published in the United Kingdom 2023
First Published in the United States 2023

British Library Cataloguing in Publication Data:
A Catalogue record for this book is available from the British Library

Copyright Chris Sutton 2023

ISBN 978-1-78952-259-4

Typeset in ITC Garamond Std & ITC Avant Garde Gothic Pro
Printed and bound in England
Graphic design and typesetting: Full Moon Media

DECADES

Alice Cooper

in the 1980s

Chris Sutton

sonicbondpublishing.com

Dedications

Dedicated to Stephen Lambe, Andy Michael and Eric Senich

DECADES | Alice Cooper in the 1980s

Contents

Introduction

For Alice Cooper, the 1970s had been incredibly successful. He could look back on a series of hugely successful singles, albums and tours which had put Alice Cooper the group – and then Alice the solo performer – on top of the world. The Alice Cooper Group with Michael Bruce, Glen Buxton, Dennis Dunaway and Neal Smith fell apart in 1974 – the first significant heavy price of fame. While his solo career looked set to at least equal the group's success with 1975's *Welcome To My Nightmare*, it had fallen away under the weight of Alice's own personal issues.

Now there he was in 1980, and to his great credit, he realised he needed to be contemporary, reflecting what was happening at the turn of a new decade. As he continued to battle his demons, he recorded four intriguing, eclectic albums, with at least one classic in *Dada*.

'The songs I wrote in the *Dada, Zipper*, or *Special Forces* periods I am not ashamed of at all. I thought it was good for hardcore Alice Cooper fans', recalled Alice in *Faces in* December 1986.

There was an inevitable collapse and time away. He returned with two metal-focused albums, followed by an all-out tilt at the mainstream with *Trash* in 1989, which put Alice firmly back on top.

The 1980s is a real thrill ride of twists and turns for Alice Cooper fans. It was certainly never dull, as you are about to find out.

Author Interviews & Correspondence

It was a great privilege to talk to so many of the musicians and performers who worked with Alice. Quite a few of them have never spoken about their time with Alice. I am hugely grateful to them all. Alice is represented here mostly in contemporary quotes, with *Dada* being the only total blind spot in his memories.

The contributors were Linda Albertano, Tommy Caradonna, Ernie Cefalu, Paul Chiten, Trace Devai, Sylvia Dohi, Dennis Dunaway, Arti Funaro, Franne Golde, Andy Goldmark, Diana Grasselli, Franz Harary, Bob Held, Duane Hitchings, Prakash John, Danny Johnson, Rick Johnson, Eric Kaz, Donnie Kisselbach, John McCurry, Gregg Mangiafico, Guy Mann-Dude, Ken Mary, Devon Meade, Susan Michelson, Jonathan Mover, John Nitzinger, Mike & Valerie Pinera, Al Pitrelli, Kane Roberts, Karen Russell, Alan St. Jon, Ross Salomone, Pepa Sarsa, Rudy Sarzo, Graham Shaw, Neal Smith, Billy Steele, Paul Taylor, Tom Teeley, Joseph Turano, Jan Uvena, Geoff Westen and Kip Winger.

1980 – Roadie And Flush The Fashion

Roadie (Warners, June 1980)

Prior to *Flush The Fashion*, Alice starred in the film *Roadie* along with Meat Loaf and Blondie. Alice appears mostly in a mini live concert setting with onstage and soundcheck footage. 'Pain' is the best here being a full live concert version. 'Road Rats' is only a short piece from the soundcheck, but does appear full-length on the soundtrack album. Part of 'Only Women Bleed' (recorded at the soundcheck) appeared in the film only. Fred Mandel says these recordings were the first steps towards an album. 'We originally started with Todd Rundgren. We did a few songs and merged the two bands, Utopia and Alice's band, which was Davey and myself at that point. Todd was producing with Willie Wilcox was on drums, Kasim Sultan on bass and Roger Powell on keyboards and synthesiser. I played piano and guitar'.

The *Roadie* songs are a curious hybrid that look both backwards and forwards – two reworked oldies in 'Only Women Bleed' and 'Road Rats' and a new song in 'Pain'.

'Pain' has only ever been released on the soundtrack album and is a cleaner, less 'painful', interpretation of the song than on *Flush The Fashion*. The sparser production works well. Todd Rundgren uses sound effects to enhance the key lines of the baby crying, the convict frying etc. Alice adopts a more forlorn vocal for this version. In many ways, it would have been a better fit for *Flush The Fashion*. Davey Johnstone's solo is a case in point, searing and cutting through the sound palette more effectively that he does on *Flush The Fashion*.

'Road Rats' is a real curio. It's a trebly, faster and two minutes shorter version of the *Lace And Whiskey* track. It's a messy version too. Johnstone's take on the main guitar riff is unpleasant, but Alice handles the vocal lines well, while the gang chorus is amusing. The section (0:53) which opens 'We're the men behind the man, we're the backbone muscle clan' makes good use of backing vocals to sound like the roadies joining in. It was released on the soundtrack album and then on the *Life And Crimes* box-set.

Flush The Fashion (Warners)

Personnel:
Alice Cooper: vocals
Davey Johnstone: lead guitar

Fred Mandel: keyboards, guitar, synth, backing vocals
John 'Cooker' Lopresti: bass
Dennis Conway: drums
With:
Roy Thomas Baker: drum machine on 'Talk Talk', 'Clones', 'Leather Boots', 'Aspirin Damage',
Flo & Eddie, Joe Pizzulo, Keith Allison and Ricky 'Rat' Tierney: backing vocals
Produced at Cherokee Studios, Los Angeles, February – March 1980 by Roy Thomas Baker
Release date: 28 April 1980
Highest chart places: UK: -, USA: 44
Running time: 28:29

> Both my look and sound are a change for the '80s. A change back to a simpler, cleaner, even starker image. The '70s were overproduced in every way. I think that people are sick of that and ready for a change.
> **Alice to** *World Of Velvet*, **May 1981**

The plan to record the album with Todd Rundgren and Utopia was abandoned. 'Alice made the decision to go with Roy. So then we started recording at Cherokee with the band on the album', says Mandel.

It had been a long time since Alice recorded an album with the same musicians on every track. The only musician new to Alice was John Lopresti, who had played bass with Elton John. The connection with Davey Johnstone and Dennis Conway (fellow Elton alumni) led to his involvement. Originally Dee Murray (also from Elton's band) had been approached to play bass. He told Dave Thompson (*Alice Cooper: Welcome To My Nightmare*) that, 'Roy impressed upon us what this was, less of an album and more of a rescue mission'. That's a harsh judgement, but there is little doubt that Baker's input was massive.

The bulk of the writing fell on Johnstone and Mandel. Mandel had no previous writing credits with Alice, so this was a big step-up: 'Somebody had to do it. I ended up doing a lot of the writing. We agreed a three-way split on the compositions. It was usually a title, for example, I had the title for 'Pain', no lyrics, for 'Model Citizen' and the other songs too. Then partial phrases or ideas, then some lyrics and then building from that onwards. Davey and I would cement the arrangements at my apartment. I had been playing keyboards, but for this album and tour, I switched to guitar because I wrote all the music (except 'Pain') on guitar. I was trying to write a rock album. Somehow it ended up sounding new wave, which was not my intention personally. I had eight tunes written for that record. Six made the record, with two carried over for *Special Forces*'.

The number of songs by outside writers raises concerns as to whether Alice's song-writing well was running dry, as was the sequencing, which highlighted those concerns with no Alice credit until track three ('Pain'). The thinking seems to have been to bring in better songs that still suited the project than the two Johnstone/ Mandel tunes that were held over. Mandel charitably says that 'Things were somewhat chaotic. By the time we went in the studio, Alice was still writing lyrics, and they brought in other people's tunes, 'Clones', 'Talk Talk', 'Leather Boots' and 'Dance Yourself To Death'. It seems that 'Clones' and 'Leather Boots' were the replacements for 'Prettiest Cop On The Block' and 'Don't Talk Old To Me'. Neither of the latter two were recorded, but there was still enough space left to have included both! This is a short album, but clearly, the feeling was to go for ten tracks to keep things urgent. This they achieved, but why not use the two rejected songs as B-sides? Mandel points out there were other songs that could have been worked up too: 'I had recorded a couple of ballads, because I was trying to come up with something in the tradition of 'Only Women Bleed'. 'It Rains' was recorded by Davey, Dennis, Dee and myself, but it never made the record. I wrote it entirely on my own for Alice. Another song was 'My Machine'.'

Mandel switching to guitar meant working out parts with Johnstone: 'Davey and I both played rhythm. We would cut the tracks with double guitars, Davey played his Les Paul with me playing my Strat (which I bought from Alice). Davey played all the lead parts. I was handling keyboards, synthesiser and guitar. Davey and I worked on the arrangements, so we didn't go in cold to the studio'.

Most of the new wave-style tracks are on side one, while side two is more of a standard rock vein. 'Model Citizen' or 'Grim Facts' would have been better used opening side two. 'Nuclear Infected' just doesn't quite cut it as a side opener. The album ends on a low-key note with 'Headlines'. It does, however, deal with the primary sources of several of the song titles. Alice told *Kerrang* in 1984 that: 'One of my biggest influences was the *National Enquirer*, a kind of *Titbits* from hell. Especially the old *Enquirers*, because they're the ones that are more creative. Some of my songs have been directly lifted from headlines! If I was given the choice of reading something with the headline 'America ponders world situation' or 'boy trapped in cupboard eats dog', I know which one I'd go for!'

Alice told *Trouser Press* (July 1980) that: '*Flush the Fashion* is much harder, much more Cooper-esque (than *From The Inside*). I hooked up with Roy Thomas Baker, who had produced Journey, Cars and Queen. I knew that we'd hit it off as soon as he told me that he owns 22 TV sets. He's into all types of gadgets and mechanical things. We were able to work well together. He captured exactly the sound I wanted. The album is crisp, almost live. There is very little overdubbing'.

Baker also programmed the drum machine (used throughout side one). Mandel says, 'That was a Roy production idea; he had one of the little drum machines that were around then. He was a huge organiser so he set up the tracks ready for Alice to come in and sing. He helped direct the tracks a lot. He had an unorthodox recording method using a 40-track Stevens machine. The guy Stevens was in jail and if there was a problem, Roy had to call the prison to get him to help with the technical details. We were in the studio for about a month. Everything was pretty much cut live off the floor, except for the synthesiser stuff'.

Alice was pleased with the final result, telling *Song Hits* (November 1980) that: 'The concept was in the sound, a kind of cleanness. It really is just one band all the way through. It's functional. The title, for instance, came out of the sessions. I was trying to say, 'get rid of the crap,' the fills and the overdubs, you know, flush the fashion'. In simpler terms, Mandel saw it as 'An out with the old in with the new analogy'.

The cover package was key in presenting the 'new' Alice, but while Jonathan Exley's photographs of Alice on the back cover and inner sleeve are outstanding, the front cover is a dour unappealing waste. Far better to have used one of Exley's shots on the front, which absolutely gets across that this is Alice for the 1980s.

It's a mixed album. A new Alice and some of it is very good to excellent. It has an attack and freshness that was needed at the time and is a lot better than it's often given credit for.

'Talk Talk' (Sean Bonniwell)

'That was Alice's idea to do that track. It made a good contrast' (Mandel).

A great opening track, exciting and punchy with vintage Alice vocals. It was originally recorded by The Music Machine in 1966. Writer Sean Bonniwell was their lead singer. Fledgling Cooper Group band The Spiders loved the song – a recording exists of them performing it. So when Alice wanted something to kick start his 1980s output, this was perfect. It has an abrasive hard-hitting attitude and the lyrics were a wry summary of where he was at, 'Now here's my situation, and how it really stands, I'm out of circulation, I've all but washed my hands'.

It opens with grinding twin guitar riffs from Johnstone and Mandel. As soon as the bass and drums come in, you can hear this is a raw, stripped-down approach that Alice has not had in a long while, as far back as *Love It To Death* or *Killer*. Alice is immediately on form, grabbing the song and performing the lyrics with real purpose. The only frippery in the mix is the drum machine, which is a low pulse in the background.

The ever-busy Mandel overdubs a lead synth part (1:02) based on the melody line, which is a lovely switch instead of a guitar fill and keeps an up-to-date sheen on the sound. For long-time Cooper fans, a throwback to past glories comes at 1;18 with a trademark 'Oh, Oh yeah' that again reiterates he is back in business. For the outro, Johnstone plays a fill, riffing on the song's melody line before the staccato vocal ending. The drum machine is intelligently brought up in the mix here to smooth the segue into 'Clones'.

'Talk, Talk' was released as a single, backed with 'Dance Yourself To Death'.

'Clones (We're All)' (David Carron)

'You know, I don't really like 'Clones'. When Roy Thomas Baker played it for me, I liked it, but my opinion has changed since then'. So said Alice to *Live!* in June 1982. Clearly, the song's attraction had gone for him after playing it live for two years, but his opinion softened and he brought it back on several later tours.

Writer David Carron's clothes designer girlfriend Wendy Barrier paved the way for 'Clones' being recorded by Alice. Davey Johnstone loved her clothes and visited their home. He and Carron hit it off, jamming together, with Johnstone taking a special liking to the song. He took it to Alice and Baker, who both thought it was perfect for the album. 'I liked it', says Mandel, 'It was very Gary Numan-ish. It was the best single for the time. I played synthesiser. 'Clones' helped propel that album'.

Baker's drum machine opens the song with Johnstone's guitar wails, joined effectively by Mandel's equally wailing synth. Alice's voice is put through a vocoder to give it a clipped robotic tone, while the twin rhythm guitars give things a tight roughness. Conway and Lopresti keep things simple, playing along with the drum machine.

What a great chorus it is, too, supremely catchy and very pop. Alice double-tracks his vocals, singing rather than speaking the lyrics as he does in the verses. At times he is joined by the backing singers, whose contributions throughout this album are superb. Johnstone gets in a backwards guitar fill at 2:18, which adds to the quirky feel before the outro, where the song fades out as the rhythm slows down.

'Clones' is another high spot on the album, a generally well-received major change in direction for Alice. It was released as a single backed with 'Model Citizen'.

'Pain' (Cooper/Johnstone/Mandel)

Mandel: 'It's like a Samba with the Latin undertones, but it's an ominous tune. It's got some classical structure to it with the piano figures. I was incorporating that with a rock approach. I sang the solo melody to Davey. I had the whole thing structured in my head and it was the only song I wrote on piano for the album. I did all the orchestral stuff on it. Alice had those lyrics prepared before we went into the studio. 'Pain' was cut with one guitar, and we had piano instead of second guitar'.

The best song on the album. Mandel's swaying Samba melody lines are a joy and offer a dynamic contrast to the lyrics, expertly delivered by Alice. We have had three completely different songs now, and this one sees Alice returning to familiar, lusher territory.

Mandel's opening piano would have pleased Bob Ezrin. That swaying samba comes in right after it, punctuated by Conway's booming bass drum. There are two rhythm guitar tracks underpinning the sound, but otherwise, it's the keyboards that dominate.

Alice hits a peak with a delivery that is up there with anything he has ever done. His vocal changes to suit the narrative – almost a lullaby for the baby crying, stinging nastiness for the convict frying etc. Johnstone adds screaming lead lines for the chorus, leaving Alice to almost croon the words!

The middle eight sees Alice up closer and personal – 'And it's a compliment to me to hear you screaming through the night'. The change of pace here is augmented by Johnstone's tasteful solo which complements the keyboards well. Both Johnstone and Mandel get another chance to shine (at 2:42) with an instrumental break that again stays with the song's melody line.

The outro is clever, dropping down to Alice, the piano and synth, then slowly fading out to nothing. Your ears strain to catch the dying sounds, only to be assaulted by the sharp incoming rush of 'Leather Boots'.

'Leather Boots' (Geoff Westen)
The shortest song Alice had recorded ('Street Fight' excepted) since
Pretties For You. We get a fizzing ball of energy that ties in strongly
with the new wave feel that permeates the album. Contrasting with the
sawing rhythm guitars, Johnstone plays a jangling guitar lick over the
top, while Alice delivers a kind of neurotic Elvis vocal, dropping into
mock villainy for the 'hurt somebody' refrain. Meanwhile, the amusingly
deadpan backing vocals sound like Flo & Eddie alone. Equally fun are
the drum machine interjections that pop up. It's one of the weakest
tracks on the album, but an entertaining listen.

Geoff Westen recalls how he got involved: 'It was being recorded just
around the corner from where I was living and they needed one more
track. Dennis Conway, one of my best buds, suggested they get in touch
with me because I was a great writer and close by. I had current things
I was working on, a treasure chest of ideas and partially finished songs.
'Leather Boots' was just a 1:51 snippet of a song idea, a guitar, bass,
vocal demo. I sent it over. They liked it and recorded it on the spot. They
called me a few hours later to tell me it was going to be on the album.
It seemed appropriate that Alice could do an edgy version of a song
depicting mayhem in the streets. If the song inspired Alice in any way,
then terrific!' It didn't inspire Mandel, though: 'It was a strange kind of
throwaway tune. I wasn't really impressed with it as far as where it fitted
into the picture'.

'Aspirin Damage' (Cooper/ Johnstone/ Mandel)
Side one ends with this paean to the perils of over-the-counter
medication. You can clearly hear what Mandel thought the album was
going to be on this one. There are the crunching rhythm guitars giving
the song its weight, which Conway punctuates with powerful drumming.
The problem is the overly lightweight feel of the song other than that.
There's an annoying synth line that bubbles away, while the verses and
chorus are dull and repetitive. It feels all rather underdeveloped.

'Nuclear Infected' (Cooper/ Johnstone/ Mandel)
Side two gets off to a bright start. The guitars are turned up on full blast
and Mandel plays some great breezy synth to conjure the spreading
infection. Alice is totally at home with the lyrics, audibly having fun:
'When I'm happy I glow yellow, when I'm sad I glow blue, and I glow
red hot when I'm in bed with you'. Big respect again to Flo & Eddie for

another great backing vocal track. It's another brisk thrash of a track with no fat on it at all, lean, mean and fun, but it could have been better. In our interview, Mandel played it for me the way he wrote it, a choppier heavy guitar riff driving it along. If they had gone with his vision, this would have really rocked out.

'Grim Facts' (Cooper/Johnstone/Mandel)

'That was primarily a Davey Johnstone composition. I had little to do with that one. He came in with a pretty full track on that' (Mandel).

The sleaze is turned up high on this exciting grinding rocker. Johnstone's input is strongest and it's his chattering riff that opens it. The layers of rhythm guitars and some piano/keyboard hooks give this a great foundation. It's also one of the best tracks for Conway and Lopresti, who are locked into a terrific tight groove. On the solos, Mandel gets in some rock 'n' roll piano and Johnstone's lead parts are well-judged. Alice, needless to say, has a whale of a time with the lyrics sounding on top form. 'Strictly S.R.O.', by the way, is short for standing room only. This is one of the stand-out cuts by a long way.

'Model Citizen' (Cooper/Johnstone/Mandel)

'Model Citizen' has some strange timing things for Alice. It's 5/4 timing at the beginning, then it goes to 4/4 and then back into 5/4', says Mandel. He demonstrated to me how he thought it would turn out and, as before, it would have been a raunchier dirtier vibe had they gone down that route, but even so, this is a great, completely mad track.

Everything is a heady rush of thrills and spills. It cuts in with barely a pause from 'Grim Facts', Conway's drums kicking and pushing a very catchy rhythm, joined by the rhythm guitars and bass with the song's hook. The sparkling, lively lyrics plus an inspired performance by Alice give everything an infectious happy feel, supported by wonderfully warm keyboards. Johnstone's tortured guitar squeals are a great addition, diluting the sweetness. The chorus is clever as the backing vocalists proclaim his model citizen status while Alice sneeringly makes it clear it's all a front.

The killer part comes with the line, 'They'd like to kill me slow, Bury me deep, In the heart of Texas'. The end payoff melody from the song 'Deep In The Heart Of Texas' is delicious. 'That was Alice's idea', says Mandel. Almost as delicious is, 'I'm a friend of Sammy Davis, casually', just brilliant! The song was a highlight of the early 1980s live shows.

'Dance Yourself To Death (Cooper/ Frank Crandall)
'Very Stonesy. It's a traditional rock tune and I think it would have fit in if the other tunes weren't so new wave-ish. I like the feel and the groove on it. It was fun playing it. It was another one that kind of popped into the repertoire because I had eight songs already. Ironically it was closer to the feel I was aiming for' (Mandel)

Alice wrote this with his brother-in-law, who also worked with Michael Bruce on the demos he recorded for what became *Rock Rolls On*. The song does have a Rolling Stones vibe to it, with Johnstone's lead guitar catching the Stones' swagger. The bass and drums keep things moving, with Lopresti coming up with excellent wandering bass runs. If there's a downside, it's with the lyrics and Alice's delivery. He sounds too forced and the content is uninteresting. The chorus doesn't hit home, either.

'Headlines' (Cooper/ Johnstone/ Mandel)
It's a meat-and-potatoes rocker right from the opening stuttering guitar riff, which is great. The band are on fire with some great chops. It's interesting that Conway and Lopresti are far more prominent on side two. Mandel observes that it was, 'Based on a whole rhythm thing from Toronto, influenced by Dominic Troiano's (from the Guess Who) guitar playing. Davey came up with the chorus part'.

It's not an A-grade track in spite of the band. Alice sounds a little under par, other than the irrepressible, 'Just don't spit on me'. There's a vacuum in the heart of things, an empty space where you feel there needed to be more going on. It means the album cools down on the last track rather than going out with a statement.

Flush The Fashion Tour
4 June 1980 (El Paso, Texas) to November 1980 (Mexico)
Typical setlist: 'Elected (intro)', 'Model Citizen', 'Grim Facts', 'Go To Hell', 'Guilty', 'Pain', 'I Never Cry', 'Talk Talk', 'I'm Eighteen', 'Gutter Cat Vs The Jets', 'Only Women Bleed', 'Clones', 'Nuclear Infected', 'Under My Wheels', 'Dance Yourself To Death', 'Road Rats', 'Elected', 'School's Out'
Also played: 'Raped and Freezin'' (on at least one date in Mexico)
Musicians: Mike Pinera (guitar), Fred Mandel (guitar, keyboards), Duane Hitchings (keyboards, guitar), Erik Scott (bass), Ross Salomone (drums), Dennis Conway (drums on Mexico dates)
Performer: Sheryl Cooper

Alice was clear that he wanted the changes on *Flush The Fashion* to extend into the stage show, telling *Song Hits* (November 1980) that: 'In the past, I was known for my horror show dramatics. When Alice came to town, it was an extra Halloween. Now I'd like to try for a more Hitchcockian approach. I've developed my sense of pacing and dramatics. I want to make the audience feel insecure first, then devastate them'.

Alice's band, dubbed Hostage Fever, were pros from his own generation, all of them top-drawer players. Fred Mandel 'knew' the show and was the de-facto band leader.

It was, however, new drummer, Ross Salomone, who recruited the rest of the band: 'I had moved to LA, and I was sending my resume out looking for work. I got a call from Alice's office saying that they needed a complete band, so would I be willing to put a band together fast?' Salomone said yes and set about consulting his address book: 'I called Duane Hitchings, Mike Pinera and Erik Scott. These guys all have a great track record. We listened to a few songs, then went to audition for Alice. He listened to us, saying, 'Now that's what I want my band to sound like!" Duane Hitchings confirms that it was Salomone who got the band together: 'I heard about it from Ross Salamone, the drummer, who was a dear friend of mine'.

How the band was put together is hazy for Mandel: 'I don't know where Ross came from, and I didn't know Duane either. I was the only one who knew most of the set. I loved that tour because I was playing guitar and it gave me a chance to break out. It was refreshing. I thought Duane did a great job with the keyboard parts. We weren't doing a lot of stuff that had intricate guitar lines. A lot of the rhythm parts required two guitars to get the power, and that was the way we did the album. I got a solo on 'Schools Out'. Duane played the string parts on 'Pain' while I played electric piano, a Yamaha. It was the only song I played on keyboards'.

Mike Pinera had already been 'tapped' by Alice, having been on Alice's radar practically since the beginning of his career: 'Alice and I became friends in 1968. My band Blues Image was appearing in Thee Experience on Sunset Boulevard and they came in (the Alice Cooper Group) with the promoter saying, 'I know these guys look a little weird; they got fingernail polish and stuff, but they're really nice guys, it's part of their act'. So he (Alice) came back to our dressing room. We started talking and he was a really nice guy. They brought sandwiches in but they didn't have any for Alice, so I shared sandwiches with him. We became friends from that point on. I said, 'I'll see you again on the road a bit'. In '80, we started talking. He said, 'You know Mike, I've gotten quite big since the last time you and I spoke much'. I said, 'Yeah, I know, you're a star, man', and he said, 'How would you like to lead a band for me 'cause I'm gonna redo all my memories so I would like you to be one of the leaders of the band?'

Duane Hitchings also thought Pinera was ideal for the band, 'I brought up Mike Pinera and he jumped at the idea. Mike and I had Thee Image and Cactus for a while'. Pinera had only one reservation: 'I told Alice I wasn't going to be able to stay very long in the band because I had my own band for solo recordings. He said, 'fine, whatever you can do, we appreciate it'. Shep Gordon said the same thing, so Duane and I joined the band'.

There was a noticeable number of smaller venues for what was a stripped-down show with few props, relying on the music for effect. Mandel recalls: 'Alice wanted to pare everything down with a military-style commando look onstage. We were in berets, torn shirts and kind of military camouflage stuff. The set was very bare. There was no guillotine, monsters or dancers, just a straight rock 'n' roll approach. The *Fashion* tracks were aimed to be played live'.

Alice chose a new look for the new decade, coming on stage in what Jane Scott (*Cleveland Plain Dealer*, July 1980) described as, 'A S.W.A.T. team outfit with a blue cap, a leopard-skin top and an American flag attached to the back of his leather jacket. His hair was tied up for most of the show, only coming down for the inevitable 'School's Out' encore'. 'Aren't you glad I didn't cut it?', he would ask.

Flush The Fashion was well represented in the set, forcing Alice to reduce the number of oldies. Only 'Elected' made the set from his biggest album. The three oldies that stood out as inclusions were the live debut of 'Guilty', 'Road Rats' still hanging on in the set, and the recall of 'Gutter Cat'. The latter saw Sheryl as the rival gang leader who was stabbed by Alice, but there was no execution for the finale.

The tour was 'Four months of non-stop touring', says Salomone. The band are terrific on surviving recordings, equally as adept on the old material as *Flush The Fashion*. Salomone agrees, 'We were very tight playing together. Newer songs obviously were not a big hit at the time. However, the audience loved all the songs'. If the band were tight, then Alice's performances were patchy. He was either trying something new for the tour and just riffing on the lyrics as he felt fit, or he just couldn't remember the words. 'Go To Hell' was one of the worst offenders. Mandel tactfully didn't notice the lyrical glitches because, 'I was in the heat of battle playing guitar, but I don't think he was doing that great at the time'.

Salomone was always introduced as 'the protection from Sicily' by Alice because Salomone's grandparents came from there. The drummer says that 'I had no special songs I preferred to play and the tour, in general, was quite easy. The audiences were always excited to see a legend. Alice was wonderful to accompany. I remember at one concert; the lights were way down with Alice sitting on the front of the drum riser. I found out after the lights went on he had Angel, his snake, staring at me!'

There were triumphant full houses in partisan Cooper cities such as Detroit on 8 and 9 August. The crowd, who got three encores, were unaware of the dramas occurring around one of the gigs. Mandel explains 'We were rushed out because there was a rumour there was a sniper in the auditorium. We were given a police escort to get us out of the area. Of course, they told us this after the show was over'. One time they didn't get out in time was at Minneapolis: 'We were tear-gassed during the show', recalls Mandel, 'The whole auditorium was emptied because of a military tear-gas canister.

But the biggest blow-up was when a riot broke out at the 60,000 sell-out Exhibition Place gig in Toronto on 19 August. Support band Zon played until 9 pm, but the audience grew restless as an hour passed by with still no Alice. Instead, on came Pinera, alone, to make an announcement: 'I did it because I was the most vulnerable', he quips. 'Alice and I were very close, so when he got sick a few hours before showtime, he said, 'Well, look, somebody's got to go out and make an announcement'. The promoter said, 'I'll do it', and Alice said, 'No, I want it to be from the band, Mike, would you do it?' So that's how I got roped in. I did the announcement. People started going crazy and screaming. I'm saying, 'I'm sure Alice will reschedule the date and your tickets will be good'. As I came offstage, the promoter yanked the microphone out of my hand and he said, 'There's not going to be another date, they either play now, or they don't play at all'. As soon as he said that, it started a riot. The roadies were running off the stage with our guitars and stuff. The crowd overturned police cars, setting fire to things. We went back to the hotel to see if Alice was feeling better and take it from there. Every channel was covering the riot, it looked pretty awesome with the helicopter shots'.

The details of Alice's illness were given as a severe asthma attack, but road manager Damion Bragdon said Alice had been taken ill with a fever in New York, so arrived in Toronto an extremely sick man. It isn't certain when Alice played his next concert, but a week scheduled for Mexico in September was cancelled. Toronto marked the end of the road for Mandel: 'It was my first time playing my home town (Toronto) and it turned into a pretty heavy deal. This was the last night of a three-month bus tour while Alice was sick. It turned into a bad scene and I decided it was time for me to move on; I did a few more gigs and then I handed in my notice. I left before they went to Mexico'.

Two additional legs of the tour were scheduled, both given their own names. *Ma and Pa Cooper's Mini Tour* was lined up for October, while *La Cucuracha Meets The Black Widow* was scheduled for November in Mexico. Hitchings had a lot more to do as he now had second guitar and keyboards to cover, with the band down to a four-piece. Salomone couldn't make these extra dates, so Dennis Conway returned on drums. The only set-change was that 'Raped And Freezin'' was added to at least the last night in Monterey due to the topical ('alone down in Mexico') lyric references.

The County Coliseum, El Paso, Texas, 4 June 1980

The show was recorded and broadcast on the radio by Westwood One. It has been the subject of numerous bootlegs. The original broadcast was padded out with tracks from the official *Alice Cooper Show* album, possibly to include more of the 'big hitters' in Alice's career.

There are several tracks missing from the actual El Paso show, but this remains the best recording of the tour. The band played the old songs in slightly more abbreviated versions, apart from 'Only Women Bleed', which was considerably shortened. El Paso has been released on vinyl and CD countless times and is well worth picking up.

1981 – Special Forces

Special Forces (Warners)
Personnel:
Alice Cooper: vocals
Danny Johnson: guitar
Mike Pinera: guitar
Duane Hitchings: keyboards
Erik Scott: bass
Craig Krampf: drums
With:
Billy Steele: guitar on 'You Want It, You Got It'
Produced at American Recording Co, Studio City, April to July 1981 by
Richard Podolor
Release date: 1 September 1981
Highest chart places: UK: 96, USA: 125
Running time: 34:51

The album was fundamentally part two of *Flush The Fashion*. The starting point came with some leftovers, as Alice told *Live!* (June 1982): 'We had written a lot of songs for *Flush the Fashion* and had some material left over. So I decided to use those pieces on *Special* Forces'.

From the *Flush The Fashion* touring band Duane Hitchings, Mike Pinera and Erik Scott were on the sessions. Joining them were session drummer supreme Craig Krampf and eventually Danny Johnson on guitar.

The songs were put together at Pinera and Hitchings' Hollywood homes. Hitchings recalls that 'Coop and I wrote a lot of songs for the album at my house in Hollywood, California. There were ideas from both of us, plus Alice. As an example, I would play a riff and then we would start on that idea'.

Producer Richie Podolor was best known for his work with Three Dog Night and there was little to suggest he was a good choice for the edgier stylings Alice was going for on the record. Much of the grit and fire the songs had were lost in the final mix.

The album came out with little publicity or fanfare, although it has to be said that there is still plenty to enjoy on the album. A primary concern is the cover is terrible – a triumph of style (and poor at that) over substance. The logo is good and the portrait by Jonathan Exley is excellent, although wasted in how it is used.

Adding to the sense of haste, the back cover listed a track, 'Look At You Over There Ripping The Sawdust From My Teddy Bear', that never made it to the final master. Then there's the keyboard-heavy/guitar-light mix. Even when there are guitar solos or fills, they are too low.

Alice's vocals are patchy. He mostly talks his way through songs and at times, sounds hoarse and uncomfortable. You can hear the problems most clearly on 'Prettiest Cop On The Block' or 'Seven And Seven Is'. It's clear there was an issue with coming up with new material; there are two leftovers, a cover version and a reworking of an Alice classic. Mandel observes, 'I was unaware that they had cut those two tracks (the *Flush The Fashion* leftovers) till after the fact and they didn't sound like what I had envisioned'. In spite of the clear problems with working up new songs, the album is listenable, fun and has a good spirit to it. Hitchings felt the sessions went well, for him in particular: 'We had a good time! I was really good friends with Richie and Bill (Cooper, Engineer). They taught me so much about recording'.

Late on in the studio sessions, there were differences of opinion between Podolor and Pinera. Pinera is philosophical and to the point about it: 'He liked things his way; whoever he was talking to had to do what he said his way. I was not really up for that. I said sorry, I'm not going to do it your way, so he said, 'OK, I've got another guitar player coming in'. So Danny came in'. Podolor, it seems, was already lining up Danny Johnson.

Johnson saw it as just another job to do: 'Richie Podolor suggested to Alice to use me. When I showed up a lot of the songs were already written, and they had decided on what they were doing. I don't remember exactly who played what, but I played a lot of the lead. Alice is a super nice guy and very smart. He changed when he got on the microphone and went into the Alice Cooper character. He said it was sort of like his little monster like Bella Lugosi was Dracula, so when it came time, he became Alice. He always talked about Alice as though he was someone else'. Johnson tantalisingly adds that they tried a cover version out when he was there, strangely it was one that Alice had already recorded: 'We did a version of 'Talk Talk'. It was really good. Alice did it great'.

Briefly appearing is guitarist/songwriter Billy Steele, a long-time friend and former fellow band member of Erik Scott: 'Erik called me up, saying he was doing something with Alice and wanted some songs. I didn't write a lot of lyrics, but I wrote a lot of guitar parts, verses, choruses, arrangements. I put some on cassette and gave them to Erik. Alice listened to them and said, 'Why don't you come to rehearsal so we can work on some of these songs?' I showed up early and Alice was there. I had never met him before, but he said, 'Hi, how are you doing'. And, I'll never forget this, he said, 'Hey, when those guys get here, let's pretend we knew each other from High School or something. We worked on a couple of my songs and they chose 'You Want It You Got It'.'

The album was originally intended to be called *Skeletons in The Closet* and was scheduled for release on 2 June 1981. That date was scrapped because the album was unfinished. Johnson explains: 'Alice invited me to go on tour, but I couldn't because I was due to do Rod Stewart's album (*Tonight I'm Yours*) and tour. *Special Forces* was behind schedule with the tour due to start, so the band went on tour. Richie and myself, along with Bill Cooper, finished the record with Alice coming in after his gigs or calling on the phone and having us hold the phone up to the speakers giving us direction'. In the end, the album was remixed too, causing further delay, and dismay for Johnson at least: 'I wasn't happy with the final mixes; they were too guitar light'. The final words on the album come from the press release for the tour, which described it as 'a profile of pro-Americanism to the point of absurdity'. Quite.

'Who Do You Think We Are' (Cooper/ Hitchings)
The song started as a demo by Duane Hitchings and it's his opening synths which set the scene, with sounds conjuring up the helicopters in *Apocalypse Now*. Hitchings follows up those rotor blade effects by overlaying spine-tingling keyboard motifs that are straight out of a horror film.

That intro is shattered by Alice intoning the title and the band crashing in with him. Podolor's production is effective here for the most part, but as will continue to be evident, the mix is biased towards the keyboards, with the guitars lower in the mix. Alice is in good voice, although he pretty much talks his way through the song, while still getting the intent and menace of the lyrics into his intonation and delivery.

The verses have a swagger and rhythm that really appeals, and the choruses are catchy. The fill that Krampf plays at 2:21 is just great, pushing things up a notch as Alice comes back with another chest-beating verse.

As well as being mixed down for the rhythm parts, when it comes to the solo (3:02), the guitar level is still puny. Instead of ripping out of the speakers, it's just too quiet, which is annoying because it's a really good solo, as is the one on the outro. Danny Johnson plays the lead parts. 'I put that psycho lick in it', he says proudly. Mike Pinera confirms the solo is by Danny and adds that 'Duane was also trying to get a guitar sound on his synthesisers'.

This is an effective opening track which promises well for the rest of the album. It was released as a single as both a B-side to 'You Want it, You Got It' and strangely also in its own right as an A-side to the same song! The single mix is quite different, with the guitars up front where they needed to be.

'Seven And Seven Is' (Arthur Lee)

This song was originally performed by Lee with his band Love. Alice's version is harder-hitting and well-suited to his voice. Hitchings has the main rhythm part on his synth, while Krampf has the job of delivering the supercharged drumming. Pinera, Johnson and Scott weave around Alice's vocal lines, with him delivering most of the song's melody. Again he almost talks his way through the lyrics sounding slightly hoarse on much of the track. You can clearly hear him straining on some of the notes, especially on the verses. The song's odd chorus works well and whatever the strength or not of his vocals, Alice does put it across well. It does work.

The sound is a bit flat, lacking dynamics, with the guitar solo again held up as evidence of that, and Alice's voice needed to be more prominent.

A single of 'Seven And Seven Is' was released to coincide with the 1982 European dates, with Alice billed on it as 'The Legendary Alice Cooper'!

'Prettiest Cop On The Block' (Cooper/ Davey Johnstone/ Fred Mandel)

Danny Johnson was intrigued by Alice's working methods: 'Alice is very animated about what he's doing. For 'Prettiest Cop On The Block', he told me what he was going to wear on stage – dressed like a cop but wearing a dress and holding a hammer'.

This leftover from Flush The Fashion went through quite a change from how it was originally written. 'The title was a tabloid heading', says Mandel. Mandel's take on it was it being a crunching riff-heavy song more akin to something off *The Eyes Of Alice Cooper*. 'I envisioned it much harder than it ended up being', he says. 'I had different lyrics for it and Alice changed the lyrics for that tune. I had something I wrote to sing the melody for him'.

This version obviously has the same arrangement as how it would have turned out on *Flush The Fashion* because it sounds exactly in keeping with that album. So what we have here is a new wave-style song, big on the synths, but with Alice again sounding a little tight and constrained on the vocals. Musically it swings and moves well, with Krampf's cymbals repeatedly crashing for emphasis. It's not one of the best tracks, but it's enjoyable enough.

'Don't Talk Old To Me' (Cooper/ Johnstone/ Mandel)

'The melodies on that could have been *Fiddler On The Roof*, strangely enough. Musical theatre in a weird way'. (Mandel)

The second *Flush The Fashion* reject is a curious beast. The chorus is catchy with a nice descending keyboard part, but the verses are a little substandard. The whole song has a demo feel to much of it and it sounds unfinished, which may well be the case. Really this is filler in spite of Alice's attempts to get some life into it. Mandel played me his original take on the track with lots of wailing guitar suiting the lyrics, and it sounded much better.

As another in a line of Alice songs about the travails of youth, this one is passable. Those descending keyboards are the best thing about it and they somehow work well as a trailer for our next track.

'Generation Landslide '81 (live)' (Cooper/ Glen Buxton/ Michael Bruce/ Dennis Dunaway/ Neal Smith)

The idea of revisiting the song to give it a makeover was a good one, but also a brave one. The original is a stone-cold Cooper Group classic and comparisons are there to be made. Deciding to open and close it with an audience track (actually, the band) was a pointless mistake.

Once the song comes in, we get the first big positive with an upgraded 1981-style version of the rhythm and melody. It's different, but you can hear the original coming through, and it works exceptionally well. While Alice had a sly, almost laid-back approach to the original, here he sounds like an older sinister figure. His voice, which has sounded as though it is struggling at times on this album, works a treat here. The tightness and rasp in his vocals give the lyrics a more persona with a pointed delivery. Behind him, the band are audibly rejoicing in playing the song; you can actually hear this in their performance because they pull out all the stops. The snap-cracking drums and the meatier guitars give things a lift and allow Alice the space to almost rap the lyrics.

The jarring part comes with the new verse, which Alice wrote 'specially' as part of the update. It isn't even remotely as wry, witty and sharp as the original verses. The big problem is that this is unquestionably the best track on the album, which speaks volumes about the new, original material.

'Skeletons In The Closet' (Cooper/ Hitchings)

Another one that was started by Hitchings. The most synth-heavy track on the album is a delicious tongue-in-cheek slice of Alice. It's fun and catchy and could have been a single; the kind of tune that makes it to being a big hit in Europe particularly. A puzzling trivial note is the song title which substitutes 'the' for 'my'. Alice sings it in the personal 'my' form, which obviously works better.

Hitchings' synths open it with a delightfully playful melody that has a harpsichord feel to it. Scott and Krampf are excellent when the main tune comes in, keeping up a catchy rhythm which Hitchings adds a keyboard part to. Missing throughout are the guitars, but on this occasion, that was the correct decision. It works without them, giving things a sparser feel.

It's one of Alice's best vocals on the album. The lower register he uses suits him perfectly and his conspiratorial performance is excellent. He gets a neurotic haunted quality that gives a real edge to the delivery.

The outro takes it up a spooky notch with the skeletons (a deliciously spectral Alice himself) calling Alice and his exasperated cry of 'What, what do you want?' which stops the song dead. This song is one that will surprise and delight anyone unfamiliar with Alice Cooper.

'You Want It, You Got It' (Cooper/ Scott/ Krampf/ Billy Steele/ Eric Kaz)

That great finish on 'Skeletons' segues perfectly with the first line here, 'You want money?' Smart stuff on the sequencing! The driving force on the songwriting was Billy Steele, who came up with the melodies and riffs. He also plays on the track, although mixed down low, but got left off the credits. Steele: 'I wrote that opening riff and played it on the guitar. I used a Marshall 100watt through a hi-watt. Then Duane doubled it with a synth, so the guitar is somewhat buried in the track. Same thing for the rest of the track with the synth doubling my guitar part. I think Mike Pinera played the flanged guitar part and there is another guitar part in there that he (or Danny) must have played also'.

There's not much to the song, with Alice singing over the wandering synth patterns and a prominent Krampf drum part; most of the song's punch comes from the backing handclaps. The melody is cool, but it needed more work on the rest of the track to lift it. Alice's voice is good and his stuttering choral vocal is a real earworm.

It is astonishing why five are credited with writing such a simple track. Steele agrees that the number seems high: 'Alice was writing lyrics, Erik Scott was helping with arrangements and maybe melodies, but I was kind of surprised there were so many people on the credits. I don't even know who wrote the lyrics or what went on behind the scenes because I wasn't there. Maybe Eric Kaz helped Alice with a line or two or something. Craig Krampf probably got credit for helping work on the arrangement. Alice was very nice about credits. If you were there doing stuff, you got credit'.

Erik Scott claimed (to *Sickthings UK*) that Eric Kaz came up with the title concept. Kaz recalls that: 'Andrea Farber, who was the studio contractor for the sessions, contacted me about contributing. I can't recall my level of contribution, but it turned out she had a lot of people working on it. That ended my spending any more time on it. I never met Alice or ever heard his recording of it'.

Steele remains proud of it: 'I like the song; it's kinda funny. When they were doing that album, Alice was doing a lot of funny lyrics. I like the synthesiser on it'. It was released at the end of June 1981 as a single, backed with 'Who Do You Think We Are' The same combination of songs was later released again with the sides reversed.

'You Look Good In Rags' (Cooper/ Hitchings)
Hitchings: 'That was about my girlfriend at the time. Not in a flirting way, but complimentary'.

The guitars are back for this one and sounding better than they have yet on the record. The guitar fills are mixed a little higher, which adds welcome colour. If the main riff sounds familiar, it's because it's a thinly veiled rewrite of Blondie's 'Atomic' from a year or so earlier. Alice's voice is tight again on some notes, but he generally copes OK.

The section (from 2:16) with the gang-style 'Rag, rag, rag' vocals is pointless, and there is this story that the clicking noises are guns being cocked to fire. That may well be so, but you wonder why they didn't use the sound of scissors, given the title. Despite the guitars being turned up, there is another missed bonus on the outro where Pinera or Johnson solos away. Listen carefully for it, It's there in the background and it sounds absolutely great. Another criminal decision to mix it down! In spite of the solo, this is another song that should have been replaced on the tracklist.

'You're A Movie' (Cooper/ Hitchings)

Alice is audibly having great fun as an arrogant General who cares little for his drone-like troops. The low-key intro is in the vein of 'Skeletons', but it shifts into being a guitar-led piece, with a decent riff, nicely doubled by Scott, while Krampf's punchy drumming keeps things moving along.

The band have fun with the backing vocals (also featuring Alice) and interaction with Alice.

In spite of these positives, it's ultimately an unsatisfying song; it is entertaining but not good enough for the album.

'Vicious Rumours' (Cooper/ Hitchings/ Scott/ Pinera)

'I wrote the song with Alice', says Pinera. 'He said, 'Do me a favour; give me some alternative punk-type stuff. Give me reality. I don't wanna play regular rock 'n' roll, give me terrible, give me this song sucks, give me anything like that. But don't give me mediocre'. I left a lot of the lyrics open, I knew that was what he liked to do. I played the solo and I did a lot of solo work on some of the other songs too'.

Pinera gave Alice a snapping adrenalin rush of a track, and it must be said his place in the order on the credits is a complete mystery – why last?

Duane Hitchings also loves Pinera's biggest contribution: 'Great song. Mike is an incredible guitar player, singer and writer! He is one of the legendary blues guitar players of that whole time'.

Krampf's drums open it with a pounding rhythm, joined by a terrific edgy riff from Pinera, who grabs the song, delivering it with sting and attack. To make things perfect, we get a sparkling vocal from Alice. He is right on top of his game here with great voice and delivery. A whole album of material of this quality would have been fabulous. The final touch of cross-fading back into 'Who Do You Think We Are' is a satisfying end to the album. It's interesting to note that the album is bookended with the two best new songs on it.

Related material
**'Look At You Over There, Ripping The Sawdust From My
Teddy Bear'** (Robbie Leff/ Billy Snell)
This was scheduled for *Special Forces* but removed after the cover design
was signed off. For many years this was a tantalising mystery for fans
eager to hear it. The title had such promise; how could it fail?

It finally appeared on *Life And Crimes* and turned out to be
completely out of sorts to the rest of the album. This horribly limp
song stands alone with a reflective plaintive Alice vocal and a
dominant keyboard melody that sounds like something from a made-
for-TV movie.

I would have questioned if it's even the same band playing on it, but
Erik Scott is name-checked by Uvena just as the song finishes.

'Skeletons In The Closet' (original acetate mix of *Special Forces*)
This turned up on the Internet with no provenance, but it is definitely
a mix worth tracking down. In general, the guitars are mixed higher,
which is a great result, so consequently, the sound is thicker with a
cutting edge on the riffs, which is noticeable right from the first track.

'Who Do You Think We Are' is the single version of the song and is
way better. Clearly audible at 1:20 (when Alice sings 'carnivorous') is
some choppy, almost reggae-style rhythm guitar. 'Seven And Seven Is' is
ten seconds longer and the pulse synth is way up in the mix. 'Generation
Landslide 81', by contrast, is shorter without the audience noise. 'Vicious
Rumours' is also shorter, missing the sound effects.

Special Forces Tour
**20 June 1981 (Concord, California) to 27 February 1982
(Strasbourg, France)**
Typical setlist: 'Who Do You Think We Are', 'Model Citizen', 'Go To Hell',
'Guilty', 'I'm Eighteen', 'Cold Ethyl', 'Only Women Bleed', 'No More Mr Nice
Guy', 'Clones', 'Under My Wheels', 'I Never Cry', 'Grim Facts', 'Pain', 'Billion
Dollar Babies', 'Generation Landslide', 'Who Do You Think We Are? (Reprise)',
'School's Out'
Occasionally played: 'Seven And Seven Is', 'Vicious Rumours (reprise)'.
Trivia: The band broke into an instrumental version of 'Skeletons In The
Closet' at the Birmingham Odeon soundcheck.
Musicians: Mike Pinera (guitar), John Nitzinger (guitar), Duane Hitchings
(keyboards/guitar in North America), Wayne Cook (keyboards in Europe),

Erik Scott (bass), Jan Uvena (drums)
Performer: Sheryl Cooper

Alice and Sheryl's daughter Calico was born on 19 May, but her parents were back to work in June for the start of the American leg of the *Special Forces* tour.

The band were dressed as mercenary guerrillas in keeping with the theme loosely explored on *Special Forces,* and were named after the album. They represented the last group of musicians Alice would use on stage who were from his own generation or near enough. From 1986 onwards, it has nearly always been younger musicians in the band (with the likes of Steve Hunter an honourable exception), with Alice vampirically feeding off their energy.

That's not to say the 1981/82 tour band had no energy. The stripped-back edited arrangements worked and Alice had two killer guitarists on board. Danny Johnson was unavailable, as noted. You might have expected Erik Scott to suggest Billy Steele for the role of second guitarist, but no. 'I don't think it was Erik's choice', says Steele, 'because he would always recommend me, so I guess it was Alice's choice'. Scott turned instead to John Nitzinger, who had worked alongside him on Carl Palmer's 1PM album in 1980. Nitzinger recalls: 'Erik called me to audition for Alice so I went out to LA and got the job, mainly because of my songwriting. Erik Scott was the nicest guy, a good friend and a real organised guy. He put me up in LA, letting me stay at his place while we worked on the songs together and I learned the parts'.

The blend of Pinera and Nitzinger was inspired, with the two combining well with a real bite and attack that suited the concept of the show. 'We sure worked great together', says Pinera. 'We had the same roots; he had Texas Blues while I had other Blues!' Nitzinger sums up their approach: 'Mike and I split the lead parts. I was pretty much a hard-driving player. My playing's a little harder with a bluesier rock edge to it'.

Special Forces session drummer Craig Krampf turned down the touring slot so Ross Salomone was asked to return, but he was put off by the schedule: 'The tour looked too long for me, so I decided to put my efforts into building up the company my wife and I have had for forty years called Bioelements'.

Jan Uvena eventually got the gig on drums:

'I am a very eclectic kind of drummer. I was playing the drums at 16 in swing bands. I was more all-round; I didn't just bash two and four, I had a little more variety in my style. Mike Pinera was the conduit that brought me to the Alice Cooper table. Before that, he had got me into Iron Butterfly. In the midst of all that, I had met Duane Hitchings somewhere. Mike and Duane had already recorded *Special Forces* with Craig Krampf as the drummer, but he wouldn't fly on an aeroplane. So that's when it opened up to auditions. I had a shoo-in because of Mike. They already had Nitzinger from Texas and Erik Scott on bass, who had already been on tour with Alice. I went to audition and they really didn't need to look any further. We just ran through a bunch of Alice Cooper songs and they were fun, I nailed those, and that was it. They called Alice, saying, 'We got a guy, come down'. So he came down, and I don't even think he sang; we just ran through a setlist of Alice Cooper songs. He wasn't quite thrilled, not because of my playing but because he couldn't concept my look!'

Uvena proved an excellent choice, going on to become a close friend of Alice's. John Nitzinger opines that: 'Jan was a good guy and a good drummer. I remember when he shaved half his beard off, he told us, 'You get the clean you', and then he turned his head, 'And you get ..!''

Erik Scott was the band leader for the shows. Uvena says that 'we became really close friends. He helped my drumming a lot. He was like the tempo police and kept me right on it. I really grew as a drummer'.

Duane Hitchings returned on keyboards for the North American dates and the Paris TV special. The only additional performer was Sheryl Cooper, back in her usual roles for 'Go To Hell' and 'Only Women Bleed'.

To open the shows, Alice wanted something suitably eerie, so he turned to Hitchings: 'I had a Prophet synth and also composed 'classical electronic' music when in the musical conservatories I attended. Coop heard me messing around with my computer and wanted me to use it for the show intro. He asked me to come up with something, so I did. I don't have a clue what Coop was saying over it, I don't think I want to know!'

John Nitzinger recalls: 'We didn't have much rehearsal at all, only a couple of days. When we started the tour, to be honest, we didn't know the songs. Those are not your regular three-chord songs; they're pretty strange. So we learned them on the road, just trial by fire. We got better and better every show. Our very first gig was at the Greek Theatre in LA. We didn't know the songs, so it was really touch and go here or there'.

In fact, the Greek Theatre was their third gig, which makes the two dates prior to that in California look effectively like rehearsals to bed in the show, but with a paying audience.

The tour saw Alice again playing smaller venues, but his enthusiasm was undimmed. Like the *Flush The Fashion* tour the stage props and effects were kept to a minimum with no execution. These may have been partly stylistic choices, but Nitzinger's more prosaic feeling is that 'We only had a few garbage cans and stuff because we couldn't afford it'. The shows didn't suffer, though. Hitchings says the band, 'Had a good time and 'smoked it'; we went after the audience who seemed to love it when we played'.

Hit Parader (January 1982) caught up with Alice at the 1,000-seat Savoy Club in New York, a major step down from Madison Square Garden. Todd Goldstein described the show as 'An hour of barely controlled chaos where General Alice put his guerrilla troops through their paces, and threatened them with a sword if they misbehaved'. Alice explained to them that 'When somebody hires on with me, they go through basic training. If you fall down, make sure you get up and fall down again, so it looks rehearsed. That way, there can never be any mistakes on stage. Mike Pinera's great because he's always smiling and he's up there playing a killer. So Alice hits him on the knee with a riding crop, screaming, 'Are you smiling?!' I can't break character onstage'.

Pinera pushed Alice back with his own unique brand of craziness: 'We were playing a gig and all of a sudden, he got this idea on the (dancing nightly) bit in 'Billion Dollar Babies'. He pulls out these daggers saying, 'Let me see you dance' and starts throwing them at my feet. They were inches from my feet! So I said, 'Alice, hey man, be careful', but he's still saying, 'Let me see you dance'. He did it again the next night, so for the third night, I said to myself, I'm gonna play a little prank on him. I went to a joke shop and I bought some fake blood and I also bought a fake knife. I sprayed the knife with red paint. During the show, we get to the dancing part in 'Billion Dollar Babies' and sure enough, he's going, 'Come on, let me see you dance'. I said, 'Sure, throw your knives'. He throws four or five of them with me jumping up and down, but then all of a sudden, I've got fake blood over my feet, and a knife that looks like it is stuck in my toes. Alice just went numb. He looked at my feet and went, 'Pinera, what are you doing?' I said, 'Man, I'm dancing for you, I am trying the best I can'. He was, uh, visibly moved!'

Uvena got a make-over from the band: 'Erik, Duane and Mike put together this character for me like Che Guevara. They put the beret on my head, describing how this character would work in the show, and Alice bought it. It was all character play'. Despite the 'characterisation', Uvena struggled to maintain the image: 'I had such a good time and eventually, I was reprimanded because I was told I was smiling too much. Then they started saying, 'We're gonna fine you!' I mean, I was sitting back there watching this guy and it was a trip. Every night the show developed more and more, or something silly happened which stayed in the show. All eyes would be on Uvena as he played the iconic intro to 'Billion Dollar Babies': 'I guess I just managed to flail around enough, you know, to fit the songs', he says modestly.

'School's Out' would see Alice return to the stage with his hair down and the same cry from the *Flush The Fashion* tour of, 'Aren't you glad I didn't cut it?', which always got cheers. The song always features the band solos and Alice used it as reinforcement too of the band's 'military' background. Nitzinger remembers that 'We would all do a solo, but when I came out to do my solo, he would say, 'No blues!', and of course, I would play the blues. He would refer to each member depending on his mood – a Sergeant or a Corporal, but I was always Private Nitzinger'.

Uvena was usually introduced by Alice as a 'Cuban Immigrant'. 'More character play', laughs Uvena. During his drum solo in 'School's Out,' Alice would chirrup/sing along in a high pitch. Uvena laughs again, 'He did, I forgot that, and that thing we did which was so funny. He would take Pinera's hat at the end of my solo and frisbee it up to the drum podium and I would have to catch it. That was nerve-wracking because a couple of times I missed it, and he would just stop the show, go round to get the hat, and we would do it again'.

There was always a playful nervousness as Alice approached Pinera, who says, 'He had a quote he liked a lot: 'Now on guitar the Mr. Rogers of rock 'n' roll, Mike Pinera'. When he was asked why he said that, he said, 'Because Mike is crazy. Offstage he smiles like a little kid and onstage, he's lit up like a firecracker.' Pinera would sometimes throw in the riffs from 'Vicious Rumours' during his solo to tease Alice into singing it. On a few occasions, this would happen, highlighting that it deserved to have been a set regular.

In August, they played several shows in New York, one of which Hitchings invited his proud parents to attend: 'I told Alice that my mother was terrified of snakes. After I introduced Alice to my parents, he came up to my mother with his python and she went up the emergency stairs on stage, terrified. Alice's parents were there and he got a good scolding from his mother'.

Pinera's wife Valerie was also in the touring party and enjoyed it: 'I helped Alice with his false eyelashes and make-up a few times. It was a wild, fun tour'. Pinera agrees with her, finding the tour more agreeable than the *Flush The Fashion* trek: 'It was more fun on *Special Forces* because that was more musical, there was a lot more happening. It was a fun band because we wore camouflage like we were out of the battlefield or something. They were tours I'll never forget. I was sponsored by a guitar company called Aria. They gave me a bunch of guitars and that's what I used'.

But not all the party were so impressed. The touring across America was arduous, with cash flow being a regular issue. Nitzinger graphically explains: 'That was a really under-financed tour. Alice was at a low point in his career; hence we had a real cheap shabby bus and we would sleep in it to avoid getting hotel rooms. We drove it into the ground. We spun a 360 in Oklahoma City and it broke down in Texas. Me, Erik and Jan would sit at the front of the bus with the bus driver and Erik would bum cigarettes from the driver. We borrowed money from the t-shirt man to keep the tour going. The t-shirt guy made more money than some of the gigs we booked. It just wore everybody down. When you put that many people on a bus, you just get on each other's nerves eventually, so it was tough. It was a shame; it could have been something great. It had the potential to really be a good deal'.

The other new boy, Uvena, was growing annoyed by being cold-shouldered as he saw it: 'When I got into the band, Alice was already comfortable with Erik, Duane, Mike and Dan Stevenson (the tour manager). I mean, I was the coolest guy in the band, whether they knew it or not, but I was never invited to Alice's room. Alice loved playing cards, and these guys would all hang out with him. But I never spoke to him. In fact, he didn't get on the bus until everybody else was on the bus. Alice would walk by everybody, say, 'How are you?', make a few jokes, then he would go back into the stateroom. When we got to the venue, everybody left the bus and went to the dressing room, but Alice stayed on the bus'. Nitzinger confirms this: 'Alice wouldn't come out of his room except for when it was time to play. We never saw him except when he was on the stage or on the bus'.

Alice wasn't even there for the soundchecks. Uvena says the band would, 'Do some jamming a little bit at the soundchecks. Some gigs, we didn't even do a soundcheck, but it was always crisp and ready to go; our guys were great. Dan Stevenson did the vocals at the soundchecks just to check the microphones'.

When it came time to perform, Alice would not appear until the last minute. Uvena continues: 'When the lights went out, they walked him out from the bus right on stage. The only times I would see him really was during 'Go To Hell' when he would walk up to the back of the stage with the maracas, and on 'School's Out'. I was getting pissed off, this has gotta stop. So I made a joke and they told Alice, 'He wants to hang out with us'. Eventually, I got in and then it flipped. Now it became even in the middle of the night, three o'clock in the morning, I would get a phone call from him. 'U, what are you doing? Come on up'.

Despite the gruelling nature of touring North America by bus, the band didn't cancel any shows, maintaining a 'show must go on' attitude. It got tough for Uvena at one date: 'I remember playing Nashville (Tennessee State Fairgrounds, 23 September) and I got food poisoning. I was throwing up on the drum podium'.

Hitchings dropped out at the end of the North American tour: 'I had written 'Do Ya Think I'm Sexy' with Rod Stewart and I had presented the basic idea of 'Young Turks' to him, so I knew my time was going to be spent a lot in the studio with the album that was to be done with Rod'. He adds that: 'Alice was one of the nicest and most intelligent artists I'd met. He was a pleasure to work for, so we all had a good time playing for him'. Hitchings did make it over for one special European gig – the TV Special filmed in Paris.

The European leg in 1982 came as a huge surprise for fans, comprising eight gigs in the UK, while France got thirteen. Alice received a partisan reaction from his adoring fans. 'He was more popular over there than he was in America', says Nitzinger. 'There were signs all over the streets with his picture on them. I was surprised at how well-known he was. There would always be fans at the hotels'.

Hitchings was replaced by Wayne Cook (who had played with Steppenwolf) for these dates. Cook's first date was at Cannes on 26 January and he found himself on the outside of a tight-knit band. Nitzinger explains the band's indifference to him: 'He never really clicked with us. We didn't have time to rehearse again (with him), so he didn't really have time to learn much. He just had to fake it like we did in the beginning. Nobody was particularly buddies with him. It's sad but true, but nobody really liked having him in the band. It's really hard to fill Duane Hitchings' shoes because he was so good'. Uvena saw the situation with Cook as being that, 'We were a little bit rowdier than him. He was more mild-mannered'.

I met Alice and the band at the Holiday Inn in Birmingham. Alice was enormously friendly and engaging, spending time chatting to the dozen or so of us there. When he came on stage at Birmingham Odeon, it was one of the most partisan, turbo-charged gigs I have ever seen. To be there with all those people who felt like me, and there in front of us was Alice Cooper was just amazing. The old songs were the highlights, but the audience was receptive to everything the band played, just lapping up the chance to see our hero and legend in concert. The highpoint was 'I'm Eighteen', which seemed to hit a more joyous spot than anything else. The dead-stop pauses they put in at the beginning of the song cleverly heightened the tension. 'Eighteen' was the old song I liked playing most', says Nitzinger.

The last night in Britain was a rapturous show at the Glasgow Apollo. This was recorded by Radio Clyde and was used for B-sides and the later Record Store Day release of the show.

Barcelona was supposed to be played on 1 February, but it was cancelled. This must have been a last-minute decision because Uvena well remembers travelling through Spain. They ended up blocking traffic in both directions when the tour bus got stuck in a mountain pass. Uvena says, 'The police had to come. Now don't forget we got a bus full of crazy musicians and Alice Cooper on the back of the bus behind his curtain thing. Also, there was definitely contraband on the bus'. Fortunately, the wider issues with the traffic pileup kept the police busy.

After the tour had long ended, Alice was still buzzing about how it had gone. He told *Hit Parader* (1983) that, 'I never had more fun on a tour in my life. It's hard now to go out if you think you're still the champ, and I consider myself the champ. I've seen other groups that are supposed to be the big guys and I think, 'Jeez, I could blow these guys off the stage'. Uvena's summary of the tour is more measured: 'Alice was gone with the contraband. He was a very strong-minded man, so it didn't affect him. He did his work, did his job, and the band was really good. The shows were short, we were lucky if we actually played for an hour, but nobody was dissatisfied. Dan Stevenson had his hands full, that's for sure, but what a great guy. He was a really good tour manager with a lot of experience and he had to cover the cracks. That was the state of the game'.

Alice and the band (bar Wayne Cook) hung around in London at the end of the UK dates in order to record a song Nitzinger had written called 'For Britain Only'. While they were working on that Alice appeared for an interview on BBC2's magazine show *Riverside*. It went out live on 22 February, resulting in similar alarm to the *Tomorrow Show* appearance (detailed next). While Alice could cover up his issues to some extent on stage, it was obvious there was something very wrong when you saw him interviewed in close-up. One final tour date followed, Strasbourg on 27 February, and that was it. Alice would not tread the boards again till October 1986.

The Tomorrow Show with Tom Snyder, 9 October 1981

It starts with Alice bursting out of a tall steel locker for a spot-on performance of 'Who Do You Think We Are?' Uvena hits the opening beats of 'Model Citizen' as a finale. There's a brief pause before they launch into 'Seven And Seven Is'. Alice removes his jacket for a spirited rendition with him on real form.

Alice then sits down for an interview with Snyder. 'If you look at Alice on that', says Uvena, 'the way he was so frail and thin, emaciated'. Despite that, the Alice style and humour comes through, albeit mostly repeated old stories. When Snyder asks him if it is true, that he kills chickens on stage; you can't fault Alice's quick quip of, 'Oh, no, no, no. That's Colonel Sanders. Colonel Sanders kills chickens'.

The appearance concludes with a performance of 'Under My Wheels'. In the close-ups, you can see him channelling his performances of old – the inflections, stylings and mannerisms. The old Alice is still there and it's good to see. The band deliver a stinging rendition of it too.

The Capitol Theater, Passaic, New Jersey, 10 October 1981

This concert is easy to find on Youtube and exists in an abbreviated black-and-white version as well as a full-length colourised version. It's a multi-cam shoot and the sound is excellent, making it the best record there is of the *Special Forces* tour. Sheryl does not appear in the footage at all, but Alice does point and refer to her in 'Go To Hell'.

Paris TV Special, December 1981

'Generation Landslide '81', 'Under My Wheels', 'Clones', 'Pain', 'Seven And Seven Is', 'Prettiest Cop On The Block', 'You're A Movie', 'Model Citizen', 'Cold Ethyl', 'Only Women Bleed', 'Go To Hell', 'Alice self-interview',

'Vicious Rumours', 'Eighteen', 'Billion Dollar Babies', 'School's Out', 'Who Do You Think We Are'

The premise was for Alice and the band to mime to some songs on location while others were recorded in a live concert in the studio setting. Recording took about a week in early December 1981. Duane Hitchings briefly returned on keyboards: 'I had a ball on the Paris taping except getting sick for a couple of days. I think I ate half of Paris!'

When they got to Paris, what surprised John Nitzinger was the complete lack of preparation or direction from Alice: 'He would not communicate with anybody. He wouldn't tell the producer what the song was about. I wound up explaining to the producer what the song was and what it was about and what locations we ought to use'. Uvena concurs that there was no preparation: 'Nothing planned, like I mean *nothing* planned. Alice would come up with these ideas in his Winnebago. When we did 'Clones' he came up with this idea of red tubing and silver gaffer tape. He had Dan (Stevenson) and Renfield wrap him up in tape. The director, who was doing the video, she's going around saying, 'Oh, he's a genius'. He put on that big camouflage thing where all of us are turning our heads'.

'Generation Landslide '81' opens the film, shot at the Pompidou Centre, brimming with attitude and also amusing with the band posing. Uvena points out, 'When we go up the escalator, you'll see I got my sunglasses on; coming down, I don't have my sunglasses. There was no continuity'.

The band pitched in with ideas. Nitzinger gives an example: 'It's like 'Prettiest Cop On The Block'. I suggested we should go to the Red Light district. We went down there and when they saw us coming, with the cameras, sound and all that, they locked their doors'. Uvena adds, 'That was so cool, the way they cleared that street and we came up in the car to get out'.

For 'Go To Hell, ' Alice had the idea to film at Notre Dame, but permission was unobtainable. Strangely Sacre Coeur seemed to have no reservations or were not informed. Among the audience were nuns. 'That was simply a phenomenal experience', recalls Uvena. 'It was at night; we had loudspeakers, and we got nun habits on. I'm standing there but I don't have drumsticks in my hands, so I have just got my hands together in the Amen. Meanwhile, Alice is dancing around me, poking me with his sword'. Nitzinger chuckles at the memory: 'The nuns? Oh yeah, that was wild, man. We played at, I believe, the largest Catholic church in

Paris and the nuns gave us their habits to wear. They dressed us in their clothes and I was walking around with a bottle of vodka in one hand in a nun's outfit. They had no idea what they were getting into. We did 'Go To Hell' on the steps of the church. I remember the nuns running by screaming, 'Diablo, Diablo!' It was hilarious'.

The best part of the special is the live tracks which come after the self-interview. For Pinera, it's a great record of how the band was, along with showcasing his skills: 'There's a bunch of stuff where I'm taking some solos – in 'Billion Dollar Babies', 'School's Out', 'Eighteen'. It was a good band and everyone got along real well'.

Several tracks were later used by MCA as B-sides: 'Billion Dollar Babies' and 'I'm Eighteen' were used with 'He's Back', 'Only Women Bleed' and 'School's Out' were used with 'Teenage Frankenstein'. MCA later put out *Prince Of Darkness,* a compilation drawn from Alice's two albums for them that also included 'Billion Dollar Babies' from Glasgow, although wrongly credited as being from 1976.

The Apollo, Glasgow, 19 February 1982 (vinyl album)

This was recorded and broadcast, in part, by local station Radio Clyde. 'Under My Wheels', 'Who Do You Think We Are?' and 'Model Citizen' were used on 'For Britain Only' releases, while the full Radio Clyde recording emerged on vinyl in 2021. That vinyl edition is the best recording yet, begging for a wider release on CD and download. The performance is excellent, or as John Nitzinger puts it, 'A good show. We pretty much did the same show every night'. This is the best recording of the European leg of the tour and is as essential as the Passaic set. If only it had been videoed too!

On a trivia note, Nitzinger got a real boost when they arrived for the gig: 'When we did Glasgow, there was one guy, he said, 'Fuck Alice Cooper, I've come to see Nitzinger!' He made my day'.

1982 - Zipper Catches Skin

Zipper Catches Skin (Warners)
Personnel:
Alice Cooper: vocals, synthesiser
John Nitzinger: guitar
Mike Pinera: guitar
Duane Hitchings: synth, keyboards
Erik Scott: bass
Jan Uvena: drums, backing vocals
With:
Billy Steele: guitar on 'Zorro's Ascent' and 'Adaptable'
Dick Wagner: guitar on 'Make That Money', 'No Baloney Homosapiens', 'I Better Be Good' and 'I'm Alive'
Craig Krampf: percussion on 'Zorro's Ascent' (and possibly others)
Patty Donahue: vocals (and sarcasm) on 'I Like Girls',
Franne Golde, Joanne Harris: backing vocals on 'Zorro's Ascent' and 'No Baloney Homosapiens'
Flo & Eddie: backing vocals on 'No Baloney Homosapiens', 'I Better Be Good' and 'I'm Alive'
Produced at Cherokee Studios, California, May – June 1982 by Alice Cooper and Erik Scott.
Release date: 25 August 1982
Highest chart places: Did not chart
Running time: 32:25

To the fans, things didn't appear to be so awful in Alice world. We got the European release of 'For Britain Only' in April, followed by the recording and release of *Zipper Catches Skin*. Alice was, at the time, proud of this album, telling *Hit Parader* (March 1983):

My latest album is totally kill. Real hardcore. In fact, I invented a couple of songs that were remakes of other songs just for the purpose of attacking clichés. There are no clichés on this album, and I did that for a specific reason. Rock and roll right now is jammed with clichés. The only really good writers that are coming out right now are whoever writes for The Pretenders or The Waitresses. You're talking about some good lyrics there. I believe in lyrics. It's a very important thing in this business.

The original plan was to bring back Richard Podolor to produce, which is incredible when you consider how far from his production the live band had been. Instead, it fell by default to Alice and Erik Scott to produce it, and they at least got a better sound than on *Special Forces*.

A positive for Alice was that he had a core band who had been with him through the entire *Special Forces* tour, including two (Scott and Pinera) who had been with him since 1980. Pinera is quick to stress that: 'I played on all of them, but I wasn't featured on lead on all of them'.

Billy Steele was back again: 'Erik asked me for songs, so I gave him a tape and he took it to Alice. He liked the songs and wanted to work on them'. This time he also got credited for his significant guitar parts: 'I played on the two songs I wrote ('Zorro' and 'Adaptable'). Alice was very friendly and so were the band. I played a Gibson SG 61, with a DiMarzio pickup on the treble on 'Zorro's Ascent'. Then I used a 1964 super-reverb and a Tel-Ray echo unit as a preamp. Erik would always call me up because we played so well together. Our parts would always be complementary'. The guitarist Billy was most aware of at the sessions was John Nitzinger, who says, 'I played lead on the songs that I wrote, and Mike did some parts too. He played on most of the album with me, but if it sounds like Texas, then it's me! I like most of *Zipper Catches Skin*. That was a good album. I co-wrote 'Zorro's Ascent', 'I Like Girls', 'Remarkably Insincere' and 'Tag You're It'. I remember always going to the Union to collect my checks. Those were hard-core rock 'n' roll days!'

Not referenced on the credits is that it is a totally different line-up playing on 'I Am The Future', the song being recorded for the film *The Class Of '84*, prior to the *Zipper* sessions. Jan Uvena confirms the 'Zipper band' did not play on it because 'That was thrown in on the record'. The different band line-up was not disclosed until *Life And Crimes* was released.

The sessions were run by Erik Scott, who must have had his work cut out to get it done. Alice touched on this to *Metal Hammer* (December 1987): 'When I think back (to *Zipper*), I really wish I could re-record some of those songs again. When I think of the state I was in I really can't imagine how we ever got the album done. *Zipper* was a total speed-out; everything was about three times faster than it should have been'.

Alice wrote the lyrics in hiding in the studio. Uvena elaborates, 'In the room where we were recording, they built a little tent out of gobos and blankets. That's where Alice would stay to be writing lyrics'.

Uvena is left with uncomfortable memories of the sessions: 'There were things that were taking place during the recording. The last few times I listened to it, I could hear the ambience of that room on those tracks and that actually made me feel uncomfortable. The music reflects the certain staticy vibe. When the scissors fall on the floor, I am in that room. It takes me back to a time that had its good things, but it had things I would like to forget'.

Leaving aside personal issues, Uvena feels that the songs just were not up to standard: 'I don't think any of the songs we had were like the older songs he'd done, though 'Zorro's Ascent' and 'Adaptable' are two fun tracks to listen to'.

Hitchings is dismissive of talk that the sessions were tough work. 'Nah, same old music insanity stuff!' he says. Pinera, too recalls it was business as usual: 'We had spent the quality time on that album as we had done on *Special Forces*. We composed and rehearsed. Then we would try it out on Alice. He would be like, 'yeah, I like this one'. Steele also had a happy time making the record: 'My time was fun, writing some songs and recording some songs. When I was in the studio, I didn't feel any tension at all'.

While Hitchings was warmly welcomed back by his former bandmates, it was a different reaction for Dick Wagner, who Alice brought in for his all-around guitar and songwriting abilities. 'None of us really appreciated the fact that he brought Dick Wagner in', insists Nitzinger, 'because we were doing great and we didn't need anybody else. He only played on the ones he had a hand in writing. But Alice is Alice – he does what he wants to do'. Wagner ended up leaving in frustration during the sessions. Steele recalls that there was 'A little bit of drama and he just left'.

Two female backing singers were brought in to add vocal support, alongside old Cooper compadres Flo & Eddie. Franne Golde had a great track record so came in by request: 'Erik Scott and Billy Steele were musicians I played with and they got me the gig. Joanne Harris and I were aspiring artists; she was a great singer. I met Billy and Erik through Peter McIan, who had worked with them, and they both ended up working on the last album I did for Portrait Records in 1980 called *Restless*. I wrote songs with Peter, Billy and Erik'.

The inclusion of 'No Baloney Homosapiens' with the *E.T.* reference gives us a clue that *Zipper* was recorded in May or June at the earliest. The film premiered at Cannes on 26 May 1982 and then was released in America on 11 June.

The finished album is very good once you get past the third lacklustre cover in a row. The front is a bizarre mistake. 'If you look at the cover, the lyrics to the whole album start in the left-hand corner and just go straight down', says Nitzinger. 'The album cover is the lyrics. That lets you know how fast the album was going'. The back cover photo of Alice, by Jonathan Exley, is equally uninspired, being an obvious play on the title that has no appeal at all.

The songs are mostly inspired by films and TV. The incisive wit and wordplay of Alice are well in evidence. Musically the band are tight and give the songs the right textures. Scott has the guitars mixed up and the added energy and excitement is a big plus. All in all, this is very much an Alice sleeper album, ripe for rediscovery by fans and Alice himself.

The main promotion for the album turned out to be a short film/video of Alice getting harassed in the men's room. Uvena was there: 'Warner Brothers did the advertisement and that's me in the bathroom taking a pee next to Alice. I was the first one and then the next guy who comes in, is Brian Nelson (Alice's assistant, aka 'Renfield')'.

There was no tour to promote the album. Alice was in no state to do it and the band were unsurprised. 'We all knew it was over', says Nitzinger, 'To be honest, I wouldn't have wanted to go out on tour with him again. It was not fun. Crazy shit happened on that tour (*Special Forces*) and not a lot I can say about it!'.

'It was just, 'OK, it's over', and he moved to Scottsdale', says Uvena. He adds, 'I want to make it clear the respect and admiration I have for Alice. He put me on the map'.

'Zorro's Ascent' (Cooper/ Nitzinger/ Steele/ Scott)

A terrific, fun and engaging opening song. The catalyst for it was Billy Steele: 'That's my style. I like playing guitar parts and fun stuff. Basically, we worked on the intro, which I wrote, but Alice took that melody and made it a basis for his vocal. You notice he sings along with my guitar part. My original track was called something like 'Number Four' on the tape! That's what all my instrumental tracks were called, number one, two, three etc. So they would call me up and say, 'I like Number Four!' The band was me, Erik, John Nitzinger – who played the lead guitar solo on it, and Jan Uvena. Craig Krampf put some percussion on too, but he wasn't there as part of the band. I remember seeing him out there in the studio. Mike Pinera was there, too and he was definitely playing something'.

It opens with Uvena's pounding drums, tight bass and guitar before the castanets introduce Alice, who sets the scene. His vocals are really good as he uses his different stylings and approaches to give the lyrics the emphasis they need. It's very apparent that he relished performing the part of Don Diego De La Vega, aka the legendary Zorro. The continual use of percussion for added colour, as well as the whip cracks and sword swishes, all makes for an entertaining listen. 'I did the whip cracks', says Uvena, 'And there were rifles cocked'.

Another nice touch are the deadpan but tuneful backing vocals from Franne Golde and Joanne Harris.

There's a lot more to the song than is immediately evident. 'There were a lot of stops and starts in it', says Steele. 'We had to rehearse the arrangement so that we knew where all those breaks were'. What we get in effect is a shifting film soundtrack as Alice recounts the story.

Steele says, 'I played the verse guitar riff and all the rhythm guitar parts'. The instrumental bridge at 2:01 is pretty much a vehicle for brief guitar solos before a longer solo over the extended outro, played by Nitzinger, who is happy with the track: 'That was one of the better tracks, I believe. Alice had a whip for the sound effects and that was such a thing trying to record it'.

'Make That Money (Scrooge's Song)' (Cooper/Wagner)

This one pre-dates the album, having been written by Cooper and Wagner allegedly for part of a proposed project based on Charles Dickens' *A Christmas Carol,* though Susan Michelson has no records of it. Luckily it was picked up for *Zipper* and marks the first appearance of Wagner, who plays the solos. The riff veers close at times to being a detuned version of 'The Black Widow', but arguably used more creatively here.

It's similar to 'Zorro' in that Alice performs the character of Scrooge, turning in another terrific performance. Musically it's solid and muscular with a creepy, edgy feel to it, which stabs away behind Alice's explanations of just how all this came to be. There's a rough edge to his top notes on the choruses that works but hints that his voice was suffering a bit.

Nitzinger says one of the best lyrics in the song was his: "Make that money run like honey on your tongue'. That was my line, one line I did get in there'.

Wagner adds to the guitar fills throughout, but he makes his mark from 2:41 with a solo which builds up against the rising backing track. It could have done with a little more prominence because it's a fine piece of work, as is the song itself.

'I Am The Future' (from the motion picture *Class of 1984*) (Gary Osborne/ Lalo Schifrin)

'I love Lalo Schifrin', Alice told *Hit Parader* (1983). 'I love the TV themes he does. I met the guy and he was great. I agree (that) it sounded like my lyrics, except there were a couple of clichés. I could've changed them, but I didn't want to take advantage of the fact that I was producing'.

The song was actually produced by Steve Tyrell and was recorded at Jennifudy Studios and Cherokee Studios (both in Los Angeles) before the *Zipper* sessions with a stellar line-up of session musicians: Jeff Baxter (guitar), Nicky Hopkins (piano), Nathan East (bass) and Ed Green (drums). It's surprising that the musicians are not credited on *Zipper*. *Life And Crimes* was the first time there had ever been a credit for the musicians on the song.

It's pleasant enough, but it is the weakest song on the album because it doesn't fit the tone of the record. The lack of any input from Alice in the songwriting contributes to the somewhat sleepy AOR sound that dominates. His vocal is somewhere in his *Goes To Hell* era style, where he sounded as middle of the road as he was ever going to get. Things pick up for the extended outro with a lot more punch and attack in the music.

Two versions exist, the album version (mixed by Erik Scott and Dee Robb) plus a remix which appears on *Life And Crimes*. The remix (by Gabe Veltri) was issued as a single.

'No Baloney Homosapiens' (for Steve and E.T.) (Cooper/ Wagner)

A rare 'comedy' song outing for the Cooper/ Wagner partnership. One wonders if Wagner knew it was going to end up as such because there is drama in the music that is the total antithesis of the tongue-in-cheek lyrics.

It follows on in a similar sounding vein to 'I Am The Future' on the intro, but as soon as Alice comes in and stamps his authority, the whole thing erupts into life. There are nationalistic notes to the music on the choruses that hint at 'I Love America', coming up on *Dada*. The sounds of E.T. in the background are fun, with added laser beam attacks and synth swells. Sadly Hitchings has no memories of recording the track!

Wagner again stamps his mark all over it with those typical fills he is known for. He gets in a majestic solo at 3:13 that's up there with his best work, a euphoric soaring solo that riffs around the song's melody. The gang vocals that come in for the outro are amusing and lead into a chilled-out ending that apes the intro. It's an amusing and entertaining song, if not an essential one.

'Adaptable (Anything For You)' (Cooper/ Steele/ Scott)

Steele says, 'I gave Alice a tape of the guitar track I had come up with, so he wrote lyrics and a melody to my track. I played that rhythm part and I think Nitzinger played lead. It was cool to hear it. We rehearsed it through and then Alice came back with the vocals. When I arrived, I didn't know what it was going to be. It was, let's do this, let's try that. We worked out the final arrangement with Erik, and then we recorded the song'.

Steele's delicious guitar riff gives this song a swinging momentum. The way he sticks to it like glue and hammers it home is utterly infectious. Adding to the delight are Scott and Uvena, who leave spaces around Steele's guitar part. Uvena's drumming is terrific as he plays a catchy rhythm that's a treat on its own. He smiles at the praise, 'That song reminds me of the tight bass/ drum relationship I had with Erik!'

Then there's Alice. You can hear his enjoyment with every nuance of his vocals. The obvious relish in lines like: 'I'm a Sony, you're Panasonic, I'm heavy metal, you're philharmonic' is a joy. The album's running 'theme' of nods to TV and the movies is referenced in the mention of Katherine Hepburn and Henry Fonda, who play a devoted old couple in *On Golden Pond,* which Alice changes to 'Ponda' to get the rhyme to work. Should the subject of Alice's devotion fall into said pond then Alice is there for mouth-to-mouth resuscitation, which by the end of the line, he manages to turn into a sensual experience. Classic Alice!

This song is one to enjoy, savour and play a lot. For light-hearted fun with a killer swing, then look no further.

'I Like Girls' (Cooper/ Nitzinger/ Scott)

Alice told *Hit Parader* (1983) how pleased he was to get Patty Donahue (The Waitresses) to guest on the track. 'I consider her the Eve Arden of rock and roll, 'cause she's got the greatest cynicism. I'd be driving in the car and every time I'd want to turn up the radio, it was Patty Donahue. You know how, if you hear something you like and you don't know who it is, you turn it up? Four different times it was The Waitresses. Their lyrics were so funny! I requested her purposely for 'I Like Girls' and I said to her, 'Give me everything you can". The late Patty Donahue is indeed superb on this. She drips with sarcasm and is a perfect foil for Alice. 'She was hilarious. I loved her', agrees Uvena.

John Nitzinger drily picks it out as 'Another of the better ones'. He plays the song's choppy rhythm guitar, while Alice riffs over the top about the string of ladies in his life, who he 'loves to death'. At 1:10, Alice describes himself as a 'suave sophisticated lover' and an insistent castanet part comes in. Craig Krampf's percussion credit on the album remains uncertain, but this might well be another one of them.

This is another enjoyable track, all about the push and pull between Alice and Patty in a hugely entertaining duet. She gets the last words, too, with a curt 'Oink off'. It was released as a single, backed with 'Zorro's Ascent' or 'Make That Money'.

'Remarkably Insincere' (Cooper/ Nitzinger/ Scott)
With no break at all after Patty's 'dismissal', a back-pedalling Alice lurches into this high-tempo apology/ explanation of his behaviour. It's effectively part two of 'I Like Girls' but lacks the charm and fun of that track. It sounds rushed, which of course, it is supposed to be, full of nervous explanations and so on, but it also sounds a little unfinished and still at the demo stage. It works well enough because of the breathless pace, which leaves it all over at 2:07, the shortest song on the album.

'Tag, You're It' (Cooper/ Nitzinger/ Scott)
'One of my favourites', Alice told *RIP* (September 1990). He's right; this compelling song holds its own with much of what he has done before. Lyrically it's an overview of a slasher horror film from the director's point of view. Alice handles it superbly, switching between descriptive exposition and directorial instructions. The latter is exemplified by: 'We cut to you, we move in close, you're catatonic, you get a close up there'. The instrumentation enhances the mood with scary horror film tropes. The chattering guitar particularly builds suspense well. The sound effects are terrific and they must have had great fun putting it all together. Alice gets to play the part of the psycho killer calling for his victim as well, in what is a hugely varied performance from him.

The outro gives a lyrical nod to John Carpenter's *Halloween* before the pay-off line of 'Tag you're it sweetie', grimly echoing the playground game and bye-bye to poor Debbie. A fabulously engaging piece with a beginning, middle and end to rival any horror film.

'I Better Be Good' (Cooper/ Wagner/ Scott)

The song, which gives us the album title, sees Alice concerned about standards of behaviour. He runs through a series of scenarios that he had best avoid and had 'better be good'.

It's another listenable, fun track that has little of merit to it other than the interplay with Flo & Eddie's backing vocals and Dick Wagner, who unleashes his typical scorching lead guitar lines. The solos from 1:54 onwards are superb and the song is worth it for those alone.

'I'm Alive (That Was The Day My Dead Pet Returned To Save My Life)' (Cooper/ Wagner/ Scott)

The bizarre concept of the lyrics startled everyone, including Alice, who was also baffled by it. 'Man, where did that come from?', he exclaimed to *RIP* (September 1990). The dead pet in question is a stallion named 'good old Blue'. In the first verse, Blue saves Alice as he is distracted while crossing the road, then he pulls him away from the cliff edge, and finally appears in the nick of time to save Alice from Fats and his gang in an alleyway! It's all delivered as a stream of consciousness, with Alice sounding like he can scarcely believe the story himself.

Wagner gets to handle the lead guitar, while Flo & Eddie also return on backing vocals. The abrupt ending is an odd way to finish the album, but perhaps Blue didn't get there in time for a long fade-out. Still, a fun ending to what is an enjoyable and occasionally excellent album.

Related release
'For Britain Only' (Cooper/ Nitzinger/ Pinera/ Uvena /Scott)

The *Special Forces* touring band recorded this one-off song in appreciation of the rapturous UK audiences on the 1982 tour. Alice told the band about the likely reception they could expect and this inspired Nitzinger. 'We were going to Britain, so that's why the idea came to me and that's why I wrote the song. We went to the studio and Elvis Costello was there to get Alice's autograph. I thought that was kind of funny. I had different lyrics, but the title was the same. When I wrote a song and presented it to Alice, he would put his own lyrics on it and take mine off, because it was just the music he wanted. That was not pleasing to me. 'For Britain Only' and 'I Like Girls' were different with my words. On

'For Britain Only', Pinera wrote the bridge and I wrote the melody and the rest of it'.

Wayne Cook didn't play on it, but no keyboards were required anyway. Dick Wagner also wasn't there, but might have wondered why he didn't receive a credit for the snippet from 'Guilty'. Another snippet at 2:06 is a loose version of the opening bars of the National Anthem.

It's a positive, feel-good song and the intent behind it is very touching. Full credit and thanks to Alice and the band for recording it for us.

The song was produced by Alice and Erik Scott at Air Studios in London, with overdubs at Record One, Los Angeles. It came out in April 1982, backed with three songs from the Glasgow Apollo live recording.

1983 – 'Dada'

'Dada' (Warners)

Personnel:

Alice Cooper: vocals

Dick Wagner: guitar, bass, backing vocals

Bob Ezrin: Fairlight CMI programming, keyboards, drums, percussion, backing vocals

Graham Shaw: Oberheim OB-X, Roland Jupiter, piano, guitar, backing vocals

With:

Prakash John: bass on 'Fresh Blood'

John Anderson: drums on 'Fresh Blood'

Richard Kolinka; drums

Lisa DalBello and Karen Hendricks: backing vocals

Produced at Phase One Studios, Toronto and ESP Studios, Buttonville, Ontario, Spring 1983, by Bob Ezrin

Release date: 28 September 1983

Highest chart places: UK: 93, USA: -

Running time: 42:15

While there had been much to enjoy on the previous three albums, there was little about them to suggest a classic was coming. *Zipper* had its advocates, but not everyone was convinced. Then there was Alice's personal decline, which at the time was largely a secret, though there in plain sight on TV appearances and press interviews.

The only way of making a contract-fulfilling final album for Warners was to turn to those who understood Alice best, and who were prepared to work with him. Bob Ezrin came on board first (probably at the behest of Warners) to get things started. He then contacted Dick Wagner, asking him to go to see Alice in Phoenix to persuade him to come to Toronto to make the album. For Wagner, this was a huge display of loyalty and affection after his experiences on *Zipper*.

Susan Michelson says: 'Dick would keep showing up. I guess Sheryl had him over, and he sat there and wrote in the living room. Alice didn't want to come downstairs, but Dick kept writing, hoping to lure him down with the sound. Eventually, Alice came downstairs and everything took a new shape'. Despite the progress, Wagner was still unable to persuade him to leave Phoenix for a wintry Toronto until, said Wagner,

'Shep (Gordon, Alice's manager) somehow made a cheque for $90,000 appear'. (from his autobiography – *Not Only Women Bleed*).

Graham Shaw's involvement came courtesy of a project with Ezrin. 'He'd flown me out to London to do some writing for Jeff Beck. Although that project didn't fly, we enjoyed the work, so he invited me to contribute to *Dada*. He and I started working on our end up at his place in King City, Ontario. We had a Fairlight sampler about the size of a steamer trunk. Both Bob and I played on that. The Fairlight was quite a bit of fun for all of us, giving us a percussive footprint for most all the tunes. We got some fascinating other samples, too and managed to create some pretty ghostly ambience. Anything that sounds like a synth is probably me, most of the acoustic piano and a little bit of guitar'.

Wagner and Alice shared a suite at the Hilton Hotel, Toronto, where they worked on more material. The close companionship made for a time that Wagner remembered fondly. Michelson continues: 'They wrote a bunch in Toronto and finished it. Once Dick got Alice lured in, because he didn't want to go up to Toronto at all, they had a really great time. It was Dick's favourite album, absolutely, of all of them. Definitely, the one he was most proud of. They had a great time sitting and playing at the bar in Toronto'.

Shaw says, 'Dick Wagner was very solid all the way around. A good rocker and he interacted with Alice very seamlessly'. He admits that there were strong influences at work which has fogged memories: 'In addition to Alice's steady titration of alcohol and coke, plus the regular consumption of certain recreational alkaloids by the rest of our squad, recollections of who did precisely what were a trifle inexact, and in some cases arbitrarily assigned'.

Shaw was impressed by Bob Ezrin's methods: 'He had a very clear vision and a sense of purpose, and, although hilariously dictatorial at times, had a very admirable sense of what worked within the matrix of his concept and imagination married with Alice's particular œuvre. He brought it all home. The departure from the Fairlight-based songs, or using Fairlight basis with overdubbed drums and bass, was Bob's call and I expect the proper one. The fascination with the Fairlight overwhelmed the simple fact that the fluidity of live performance was compromised by the inflexible nature of a programmed drum track. I figured Ez, like me, was probably itching to just blast some performances. It was fun and is a pretty respectable body of work in its particular context'.

Alice's own performance on *Dada* is eclectic. The thin vocal style that we last heard on *Lace And Whiskey* returns, most noticeably on 'No Man's Land' and 'Fresh Blood'. He does well, but you know he could have done better. His best performance comes on 'Former Lee Warmer', which is vintage Alice, or on 'Scarlet and Sheba' and 'I Love America' – on both of which he flexes some vocal muscles.

Dada is a bold risk-taking album. The title track is a supremely adventurous start to an album by an established star. It's a deeply confessional album at times, too, while at other times is very funny. It has grown in status over the decades, and many Cooper fans, myself included, rate it as one of his best.

Another bold aspect was the cover, courtesy of other returning old friends – Pacific Eye & Ear. Illustrator Glen McKenzie did the design based on Dali's *Slave Market With The Disappearing Bust Of Voltaire*. The original concept came from company head Ernie Cefalu, who 'Shared it with Alice and Shep'.

Alice's personal issues came to a head as soon as the sessions were over. Returning home to Phoenix (circa July), he was admitted to hospital and diagnosed with cirrhosis of the liver. His weight had plummeted and without drastic measures, it seems likely we could have lost Alice in 1983. Two and a half weeks of drying out saved his life. From here on, Alice was on the road to recovery. If Alice's health was on the way back, his marriage to Sheryl had reached critical mass. She filed for divorce in November.

'Dada' (Ezrin)

Dada was a movement in art and literature based on deliberate irrationality and negation of traditional artistic values, which is certainly something Alice has often touched on. The pun on the opening track is that Dada is also a childlike familial term for a father.

This unsettling piece is one of the most uncomfortable listens in Alice's back catalogue. It's an overture in effect for the album. Shaw explains what you are listening to: 'The Fairlight is the source of Bob's daughter Sara's voice. He was like a big kid with that sampler. He also did the big booms on the Fairlight and probably the lead instrumental voice. The swirling old-time envelope saw synth is probably me. The pulse beat is a good chance of being the Oberheim and I also did certain two-bar passage resolutions. That's Alice and Bob doing the Q & A'.

That bizarre Q & A is where Alice's mixed-up personality is explored on the couch to Toronto Bob himself. It's absorbingly real-sounding and it's a relief when the claustrophobic listening experience ends on a short fade into the warmer sounds of 'Enough's Enough'.

'Enough's Enough' (Cooper/ Wagner/ Shaw/ Ezrin)

It's a contradictory track. Lyrically there's an enormous amount of pent-up and released tension in the relationship between mom's 'little cowboy' and his father. Alice rarely sounds as angry as the lyrics suggest and they are married to an 'up' and vibrant instrumental track. The keyboards, at times, are pure Broadway musical (as Shaw admits), while the only sense of torment in the music comes from Wagner's superb fiery solo.

The only let-down is the programmed drums which are too leaden; otherwise, this is a hugely enjoyable song that lightens the mood. Shaw is particularly enthused by it: 'I just started fiddling with it, channelling a cheap Canadian Leonard Bernstein. I wrote the first bit, a four-bar snippet, and came back the next day and Bob had added a bit which was really good, so then I added some more. It was truly a collaboration. The lyrics are the funniest and were, for the most part, Alice, near as I can remember, although me and Bob probably threw in a couple of lines or refinements. Dick, I think, was responsible for the middle eight'.

After the claustrophobic tension of 'Dada,' this is a well-crafted, bright opening song.

'Former Lee Warmer' (Cooper/ Wagner/ Ezrin)

This macabre gem deserves a place in the live set to this day. Shaw explains that: 'The title was a pun on Alice doing this project to fulfil a contractual obligation as I understood it'. It was indeed a pun on 'formerly Warner' as a parting shot to the label. Wagner says it was he who came up with the title originally. He added (in *Not Only Women Bleed*) that', 'I came up with (it) in my attempt to get Alice back writing again in Phoenix'.

It's a clever lyric that draws you in, with the story of a man living alone in the old family home. Well, almost alone, because his brother, the 'misconceived of the family', is 'in an upstairs room under lock and key'.

Shaw feels, 'I was a tad more present than the credits would suggest. Some of the lyrics were mine, for example. The opening and recurring

Ostinato theme, plus some chord movements were my contributions, too, as I remember it. All the ambient stuff and the drums, however, which was all fine work, I had no hand in. I think my usefulness had run its course during the final short strokes of this tune'.

That opening ostinato theme is another bit of Broadway magic, a hopeful yearning piece that leads into Alice's vocal. He sounds like he is sat in a leather armchair in a dusty old room and he sounds like an older Alice. His performance of the lyric and his phrasing, in particular, is masterful. The delivery of 'arthritic fingers' is pure Alice, as is 'yellow stained ivory keys'.

The section with the ambient effects is beyond creepy. We hear Alice going to the door of his brother's room and unlocking it with 'the master key'. The swelling rush of sound as the door opens signifies the depth of feeling between the two brothers – the last of the family. That his brother has major issues is clear as he struggles to even peep out of the window and 'wave to his father out in the family grave'. That's a classic Alice lyrical twist!

Wagner's touching, mournful guitar echoes the conflict in Alice's head that he loves his brother, yet at the same time, is concerned that he might himself end up in the same situation. The angst and conflict are still there as it cools down to the fade. Nothing is resolved – it never will be. An absolute masterpiece!

'No Man's Land' (Cooper/ Wagner/ Ezrin)

Time to lighten the mood with our hero recounting his experience 'in Atlanta in a mall playing Santa'. You have to love that he got the job, 'not because of any talent, but because I was the only one the suit would fit'! Alice uses a metronomic style at times, suiting the mundane nature of the job, albeit bringing joy to the kiddies at Christmas. For contrast, he breaks out from that to sing with gusto, especially on the choruses, where he is joined by the playful backing vocals of Ezrin and Wagner, but not Shaw, who says, 'I don't think I was even in the building for that one'.

Musically it's a jolly mid-tempo thump, with the drum machine sounding particularly leaden. The colour and sparkle in the sound come from the synths and keyboards, with Wagner's guitar also present but too low in the mix. Too low until he rips out a solo at 2:03 that riffs around the song's melody line.

It's one of the album's lesser tracks, but there is enough to enjoy about it.

'Dyslexia' (Cooper/ Wagner/ Shaw/ Ezrin)
Shaw: 'That was a pun of which Alice seemed quite enamoured – I wasn't so much. I wrote the lion's share of the music, all the synths except the drum track (Fairlight) which was cooked up by Bob and me. The overall soundscape and ambience were children of the times. All the big voices was my take on a John Lennon 'aah' chorus. The line, 'since I bumped into you, I bump into walls', I ended up singing as Alice couldn't seem to grasp the melody. To me, I sounded just awful. I'm so glad Alice subsequently replaced my voice; he sings it great. Bob did a great job on air traffic control in making the final track much more cohesive than it might have been. There is a Peter Gabriel tune released maybe a couple of years later and the bed track sounds remarkably similar'.

The song is driven along on that bed track which does indeed sound like Peter Gabriel or vice-versa. Alice is not high enough in the mix, which is a shame, as he sings it well. It's very much a product of the mid-eighties and this could have been a hit single with the right promotion. It's very catchy – another amusing listen. It may not be one of the better tracks, but it's good enough and doesn't let the album down. Shaw is right about the pun wearing thin, though!

'Scarlet And Sheba' (Cooper/ Wagner/ Ezrin)
One of the most musically ambitious cuts on the album and one of the very best. It was inspired by two waitresses (one blonde, one redhead – no names) at the Hilton hotel where Alice and Wagner were staying while recording the album. Somehow their charms were transformed into this tale of Scarlet and Sheba, two dominatrixes with intent.

Wagner's opening power chords are accompanied by suitably mysterious Eastern drones on the Fairlight, with faint clinking, insistent percussion in the background. As the music swells, Alice comes in, a beaten, adoring persona full of admiration and respect for the duo. He switches his love and attention between the two, who come over as a formidable tag team. The guitar and keyboards on the choruses cleverly set the tone for 'I Love America' with a similarly uplifting huge sound.

Wagner gets a great solo in at 3:46 that uses the song's melody for him to build off. After that short diversion, it's choruses to the outro, with a tempo change at the finale to cover the segue into 'I Love America'.

'I Love America' (Cooper/ Wagner/ Shaw/ Ezrin)

Alice told *Tucson Citizen* (December 1983) that: 'I've always been totally pro-American. I'm such a hawk. It's the kind of thing where I don't like the Russians at all. The Alice thing has always been an all-American thing, as much as apple pie'. This may well be so, but you can't take the Redneck list of all that's great in his American world seriously. It's all written, sung and performed with tongues firmly in cheeks – it is hilarious. Yet there is a warmth and affection to it; the protagonist is happy with his lot.

What is almost an alternative working man's national anthem needed a suitably big, bombastic backing and Shaw was entirely responsible: 'The music is all mine and we all chipped in on the lyrics'.

The opening salvo of drums and a power-chord homage to 'God Bless America' sets the scene perfectly. Alice is straight in with an endearingly chirpy Redneck voice that's impossible to dislike, while Wagner plays some killer guitar in the background – a heavy rhythm riff and harmonic melody fills over the top.

The lyrics are a stream of consciousness, with any verse structure being almost irrelevant, while the chorus is just the title sung with deep-voiced gusto by Alice, Ezrin, Shaw and Wagner. It's hard to believe we are only 44 seconds in when Alice puts in another appearance, as the owner of 'Cooper's carnival of clean and classic cars'.

All of the lyrics are fabulous, but you have to pick out 'I love what the Indians did to Custer!' The line cues up martial drumming and suitable 'native' vocals as the 'Indians' charge in from speaker to speaker, followed by the Cavalry retreat. 'We had a lot of fun doing the cavalry charge', says Shaw. The train sounding its horn is a neat touch, a sound that covers territorial expansion and the beginning of the end of the Native American heartlands.

The second 'choice' lyric must be the line where Alice walks away from an obvious rhyming couplet: 'I love my car and I love my truck, I'd do most anything to make a buck, I love a waitress who loves to flirt, they're the best kind'. With that, he heads off into the sunset, still effervescently happy with his lot.

I love this song for the great lyrics and the overblown ridiculousness of it. Like all of *Dada,* it has never been played live, and it may be thought too 'obscure' by Alice to do it now, but it would be sheer joy.

There was a 12" release of the song as a single that also featured 'Fresh Blood' and 'Pass The Gun Around'.

'Fresh Blood' (Cooper/ Wagner/ Ezrin)

The track is vintage Alice, a serial killer on the prowl, surprisingly a theme he had not touched on before. The decision to use old friend Prakash John on bass and John (originally Jorn) Anderson on drums made for a song that is more organic than the rest of *Dada* and a firm nod back to 1970s Alice.

Having Prakash around was a happy accident: 'I came by Phase One in Toronto when they were recording it. Next thing you know Wagner's saying come and play on this tune. Now I've never heard it. It's a different attitude you have when you're not really in the band. It just happened, grab this bass, play on it. Off I went'.

Prakash was well aware of Jorn Anderson: 'Jorn has been a good friend dating all the way back to our youthful music industry beginnings in 1968 in Toronto. He was the greatest of many fabulous drummers that I have had the privilege of playing with. There are not many drummers that better demonstrate the creative instincts and perfect execution that enhance the featured vocalist'.

Prakash and Anderson set their stall out from the start with a funky groove that Wagner embellishes with tasteful guitar. The brass section effects are courtesy of Ezrin and Shaw, although it would have worked better to have a real brass section. The main contribution for the first part of the song is the nagging catchy brass riff that is always there in the background. Alice's vocal is doubled for added effect, but even so, he is not full on in both performance or the mix. It's the kind of low-key vocal he used a few times on *Lace And Whiskey* – it works OK enough, but a stronger vocal would have done more for the song. Lisa DalBello and Karen Hendricks are terrific on the choruses, but their best work comes later in the song.

Anderson's drum fill at 2:29 heralds some slow-burn Wagner guitar over that relentless tight but loose groove with those stabs of brass still coming. Following more verses and choruses, we get a repeat at 3:58 of the sequence with Anderson again kicking it off, but this time it builds up to an outstanding finale/outro that is right up there with the best work on Alice's albums. Wagner teases with the guitar, slowly building up steam, while everything else just builds and builds in pressure and intensity. Lisa and Karen are stunning here, and there's a killer moment at 5:14 when that brass riff that has been held taut all through the song breaks free, descending lower and away, mirroring the pressure release of the character Alice has adopted.

It's a stunning piece of work and when Wagner cranks out the riffs on the outro just before the fade, you wish it would go on a lot longer. Oh, for an extended version of this one!

'Pass The Gun Around' (Cooper/Wagner)

It's a worryingly sad lyric that sounds personal and real. Alice had done confessional lyrics before, notably on *From The Inside,* but there was still an element of the performer about them. 'Pass The Gun Around' is stripped to the wires and very raw.

Wagner (in *Not Only Women Bleed*) says that the song is about 'An alcoholic and his friends passing the bottle between them, a killer as effective as a gun'. That's an intriguing thought, but the song itself is more literal to the title. It opens with the sounds of the gun being loaded for a deadly game of Russian Roulette, yet for most of the song Sonny, as he is known, is alone and ruminating on the empty hopelessness of his life. A stranger appears in his bed, who he has no recollection of and repeatedly, he implores us to 'Pass the gun around, throw me in the local river, let me float away'. It's just about as grim as things can get.

The song gets going very quickly after the intro effects, with the briefest of verses leading straight into the first chorus. The verse has Mellotron flutes on it backing Alice, nothing else is needed, but the chorus is a big cinematic production that threatens to engulf Alice. The pace builds over the remaining verses with some great work on the backing track. Richard Kolinka's drums are refreshing and subtle, with Ezrin and Shaw covering the keyboards and synths. Everyone is on board for backing vocals on the choruses for added impact, but the star of this show is Wagner. He plays bass and also contributes the stellar guitar parts. His solo at 2:05 is sensationally good, one of the best he has ever played, a ferocious burning torrent of notes that sums up the despair in the song as much as Alice's lyrics. The descent to the outro sees Wagner on fire as the choruses keep coming around again and again till broken finally by a synth gunshot. The final brief coda from 'Dada' is a fitting conclusion.

It's a superb piece of work, and in fairness, it would be a long time before Alice got close to this level of excellence again.

Possibly related recording
'Demons Of The Mind' (Cooper/Wagner)

Susan Michelson says that Wagner, 'Had this idea to write a whole concept album called *Chester Rose* about a serial killer wealthy European rocker. He sent the songs to Alice to add lyrics and he mixed them together', 'Demons' is one of those songs and only exists as a demo featuring Wagner on vocals, piano and synths. It's a slow-tempo brooding piece of work that, on the verses, uses a very similar melodic structure to 'Fresh Blood'. It's so similar that you have to feel 'Fresh Blood' came out of this, or that if 'Demons' was written later, Wagner inadvertently borrowed from himself.

1984 to 1985 – Monster Dog & The Magnificent Seven of Rock 'N' Roll

I didn't waste the three years I took off; I was renting three movies a night. I didn't care how bad they were, because it was sort of like research. In the last three years, I've actually gotten more knowledge of what Alice should be doing on stage.
Alice to *Kerrang*, November 1986

The parting with Warners was announced by *Kerrang* in March 1984. A spokesman for Alice stated he had fulfilled all contractual obligations, and added the welcome news that a deal and project with a new record company 'should be announced in the next few weeks'. This was purported to be a sequel to *Welcome To Nightmare*, with Dick Wagner and Joe Perry on board. In May, Alice told *Kerrang* about the project: 'The Alice Cooper character re-awakens ten years later after all this punk and new wave thing's been here, all these odd-looking people, and this is his reaction', explained Alice. He added that the intention was for a huge tour in support of the album. With six songs already being worked on the project fizzled out, but Alice's next one was a curveball that went the whole way.

His love of horror films saw him agree to star in *Monster Dog* (aka *Leviatan*), which was filmed in Torrelodones in Spain with the director Claudio Fragrasso. Alice portrayed Vince Raven, a singer whose lycanthropic traits become an issue on the video shoots for his two new songs – 'Identity Crisises' and 'See Me In The Mirror'. Filming took five weeks over March/April 1984, but the film wasn't released until 1986.

In 1987 Alice looked back on *Monster Dog* for *Hit Parader:* '(It) didn't have much of a plot. It was basically an excuse to see how many people we could kill. There was so much blood flying around that the cameramen had to wear raincoats. Then I ended up having my shoulder ripped off by this giant mechanical dog in the film. It was a kick!'

Pepa Sarsa (credited as Jose Sarsa) played the part of Marilou in the movie. She recalls one of the light-hearted moments in making the film: 'The character I played was a very frightened make-up artist. On the second shooting day, I had this long scene with Alice where I wanted to leave the house. His character didn't allow it and, trying to convince him, I started yelling at him and eventually cursing. The cursing wasn't in the script and Alice burst out laughing at my nasty words! The director liked my improvisation and didn't cut it, so I kept the idea. We repeated the scene and dialogue and again, Alice laughed. We did the scene again and again with more laughter. We ended up with everybody on the set laughing their heads off'.

Filming complete, Alice returned to the USA and his new home in Chicago, along with the reconciled Sheryl and Calico. Bob Greene, whose book *Billion Dollar Baby* provoked much conjecture about the original band in 1973, met up with Alice in Chicago for a piece in *Esquire*. Alice was in a forthcoming mood: 'My daughter is three-and-a-half years old now and Sheryl is pregnant again. We were living in Beverly Hills, but we just decided that is no environment to bring up children. It's crazy in Los Angeles, the drugs, the fast life. There are too many negative temptations. I just couldn't risk bringing my children up in that kind of atmosphere'. Alice added that musically he was intending to write for an hour-long video featuring himself along with some of the major 1980s metal bands. 'The video will be like *The Magnificent Seven Of Rock 'N' Roll*', he said. 'And I'll be playing the Yul Brynner role'.

Among those signed up to be the rest of the seven were Def Leppard, Hanoi Rocks, Quiet Riot, Motley Crue and Twisted Sister. Allegedly twenty songs had been worked on when the project dramatically fell apart due to two car accidents in December 1984. Firstly Hanoi Rocks' drummer Razzle was killed on 8 December at Redondo beach with Vince Neil of Motley Crue at the wheel. That was followed on 31 December by the car accident that saw Def Leppard's drummer Rick Allen lose his arm.

Alice kept on working with two guitarists. Andy McCoy of Hanoi Rocks was reported by *Kerrang* to be still working with Alice in January 1985. Another musician who joined Alice at this time proved to have staying power. He was Robert William Athas, better known as Kane Roberts: 'Our first project was going to be a kind of *Sgt Pepper's* movie thing with all these different artists. The whole fulcrum on which it balanced was Def Leppard's involvement and unfortunately, the drummer had that accident and lost his arm, so that ended that project'.

Kane recalls how he became Alice's song-writing partner and guitarist: 'I sent a tape to a publishing company, Screen Gems, who handed it on to Bob Ezrin. He saw something in the writing and then Alice came up to see me, incognito, playing at a club. I got a call the next day to go down to Manhattan and meet with Alice, Bob Ezrin and Shep. I walked into the office to met Bob Ezrin, and that was the preamble to meeting

Alice. He was sitting at this big desk with a big chair and behind him was a huge picture window with the skyline of Manhattan, so it was very impressive. He gave me a low chair, which I am sure was on purpose, and said to me, 'Kane you are 50% of a great writing team and we think it would be a great thing. We love the fact that you seem to be in good shape'. He asked me all sorts of stuff, like do I party, and at the time, I was absolutely not. When I went in to meet with Alice, I was thinking, 'here I am with people who had shoved culture in so many different directions'. I was in a room with innovators. Alice and I immediately became best friends. Within minutes we were really hitting it off. We actually drove up to a studio that day, doing a bit of work and stuff, staying in a hotel. It was a really natural kind of process. Shep was very knowledgeable and had a universal approach to life and how things go on. He was like looking at stuff from a tower; he had seen everything. A key moment was when I asked for a certain amount of money. Shep called me back, and he said, 'Hey, fella, seems like a lot just to get started. We're just gonna write and feel things out'. I said, 'You know what, I trust you'. Those three words were the best thing I ever could have said'.

Alice, for his part, had been drawn to Kane as soon as he saw him in that club. 'It was a little bit of a drive to upstate New York to a seedy bar where I was supposed to check this guitar player out that I heard about. I got out of the car and all I could hear was this loud feedback coming out of the amps. As soon as I got inside, all I could see were bodies piling up in front of the stage and this huge guy on lead guitar taking care of business during his solo. As soon as I saw that, I said, 'I don't care if this guy can play, I want him'. Turns out he can play'. (*Aardschok*, January 1987)

After the collapse of *The Magnificent Seven* Alice and Kane turned their attention to what would be the *Constrictor* album. Meanwhile, Alice and Sheryl's son, Dashiel, was born on 28 June 1985 in Chicago.

It seemed to fans as though Alice had spent three years away from music. His public arrival back looked like a cautious toe-dipping exercise as he shared lead vocals with Dee Snider on Twisted Sister's 'Be Chrool To Your Scuel', recorded in September 1985 at The Record Plant in Los Angeles.

1984 – 1985 songs
'Identity Crisises' and 'See Me In The Mirror' (from Monster Dog, 1984)
These are two of the most curious songs in the Alice Cooper catalogue. Apart from Alice's vocals, there is only Teddy Bautista on the songs, who

Right: Jonathan Exley's classic portrait of Alice was underused on the cover of *Special Forces*. It got more attention as a promo photo, t-shirt and single design. *(author collection)*

Below: Alice during the second section of the *Trashes The World* show in 1989. *(author collection)*

Left: *Roadie* is largely underwhelming. It does, however, catch Alice in transition from the 70s to the 80s. (*author collection*)

Right: *Flush The Fashion*. Alice's 1980 album has some great new songs, but a terrible cover. (*Warners*)

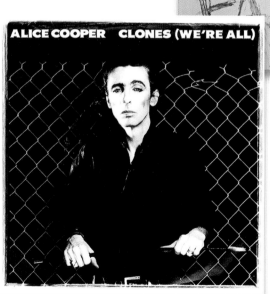

Left: 'Clones' was a new single for a new decade. It also has another great Jonathan Exley cover, which should have been used on the parent album. (*author collection*)

Right: Alice and band leader Fred Mandel on the *Flush The Fashion* tour. (*Fred Mandel*)

Left: Mike Pinera riffs it up on the *Flush The Fashion* tour in 1980. (*Mike Pinera*)

Right: *Special Forces*. The 1981 album with another underwhelming cover. The songs are a mixed bag, but it's consistently listenable. (*Warners*)

Left: Alice's appearance on the *Special Forces* tour gave cause for concern. The shows were great, but something was clearly wrong with the vocalist. (*author collection*)

Right: Mike Pinera, Alice and John Nitzinger perform 'Under My Wheels' on the *Special Forces* tour. (*John Nitzinger*)

Left: Jan Uvena and band leader Erik Scott. The 1981/82 rhythm section. (*author collection*)

Right: *Zipper Catches Skin* from 1982. An awful front and back cover, but the songs are an eclectic mix. It's a sleeper – a really good Alice album. (*Warners*)

Left: The 'adaptable' Billy Steele was brought in by his friend Erik Scott to work on *Special Forces* and *Zipper Catches Skin*. (*Billy Steele*)

Right: Dick Wagner, Alice and Prakash John onstage in 1978. The trio would regroup for one song on *Dada*. (*author collection*)

Left: *Dada*. The 1983 classic album with a great cover. Squint your eyes to see the disappearing bust of Voltaire! (*Warners*)

Right: Bob Ezrin, who produced the great run of classic albums by the Alice Cooper Group, returned to work with Alice and Dick Wagner on *Dada*. (*author collection*)

Right: Pepa Sarsa and Alice on the set of *Monster Dog* in 1984. It's a dreadful film but we did get two enigmatic songs from it! (*Pepa Sarsa*)

Left: Graham Shaw at the time of his work on *Dada*. His contributions were of huge importance to the album. (*Graham Shaw*)

Right: Alice and Dee Snider want you to 'Be Chrool To Your Scuel'. This 1985 song was Alice's first step on the 'comeback' trail. (*author collection*)

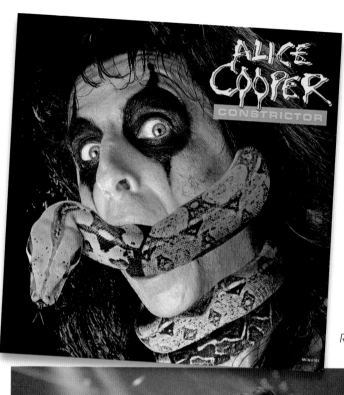

Left: *Constrictor.* The 1986 album saw Alice and his new foil Kane Roberts embrace metal. It has its moments. (*MCA*)

Below: Alice was hitting new peaks and in great form on *The Nightmare Returns,* 1986. (*author collection*)

Right: Dwight Fry has just gotta get out of here on *The Nightmare Returns*. You could tell that this was a real shock to the unsuspecting members of the audience. (*author collection*)

Left: Illusionist Franz Harary shows Alice the moves. Harary's work on *The Nightmare Returns* was an unforgettable part of the show. (*Franz Harary*)

Right: Karen Russell and Ken Mary enjoy the comforts of the tour bus in 1987. (*Karen Russell*)

Left: Sylvia Dohi and Alice during 'Only Women Bleed'. She started *The Nightmare Returns* tour as the whip dancer and 'Ethyl'. (*Sylvia Dohi*)

Right: Arti Funaro – aka Devlin 7, aka Johnny Dime – on rhythm guitar. Arti is – to say the least – an entertaining guy! (*Arti Funaro*)

Left: Trace Devai gets the point as Alice loses his patience with the photographer during 'Go To Hell', in 1986. (*Trace Devai*)

Right: Linda Albertano was the imposing and unforgettable executioner and nurse on *The Nightmare Returns* and part of *In The Flesh*. (*Linda Albertano*)

Left: Kip Winger and his buddy Kane Roberts share a moment on *The Nightmare Returns*. (*Kip Winger*)

Right: Ken Mary – the phenomenal drummer throughout Alice's metal years. (*Ken Mary*)

Left: *Raise Your Fist And Yell* from 1987. Get past the dreadful cover and there are some great songs on there, especially on side two! (*MCA*)

Right: *Trash* from 1989. The hugely successful album with a diluted Alice. There are some great songs on there, though. The cover is also the best of the 1980s selection. (*Epic*)

Left: Paul Taylor played keyboards and guitar on *The Nightmare Returns* and *In The Flesh* tours. You can also hear him on *Raise Your Fist And Yell*. (*Paul Taylor*)

Right: Desmond Child & Rouge's debut album from 1979. All four sing on *Trash*. Left to right are: Maria Vidal, Desmond Child, Diana Grasselli and Myriam Valle. (*Capitol*)

Left: Gregg Mangiafico circa *Trash*. His synths are all over the album. (*Gregg Mangiafico*)

Right: Tommy Caradonna and Alice during the intro to 'Gutter Cat' in 1989. (*Tommy Caradonna*)

Right: Kip Winger with Alice during the recording of 'I'm Your Gun' on *Trash*. (*Kip Winger*)

Left: Guy Mann-Dude was brought in to add some metal to *Trash*. His exciting guitar work is one of the album's highlights. (*Guy Mann-Dude*)

Left: Paul Chiten is one of the several synth/ keyboard players on *Trash*. (Paul Chiten)

Below: John McCurry circa *Trash*. 'Poison' (and particularly its solo) is among his favourite work in his career. (*John McCurry*)

Left: Al Pitrelli's lead guitar dazzled audiences during *Trashes The World*. (*author collection*)

Right: Devon Meade during dress rehearsals for *Trashes The World*. (*Devon Meade*)

Below: Jonathan Mover and Alice onstage in 1989. (*author collection*)

plays or samples everything. Bautista also produced and engineered the songs too at an unnamed studio in Madrid.

In spite of his considerable contributions, one thing that Bautista apparently did not do was co-write the songs, making them the first solo writing credits for Alice since 'Second Coming' off *Love It To Death*. Both songs suffer from a low-fi production, sounding barely more than demos, but each has something to offer. Both were finally released on *Life And Crimes*.

'Identity Crisises' is a surprising track. Musically it's very catchy with rhythmic syn-drums, swinging guitar fills and a low bass pulse. All of it is served up in an echoey '50s garage sound that works well. Alice sings around the riffs in the spaces, for the most part using little style in his performance. He has that basic no-frills quality here, though he pushes harder on the choruses. It's not a classic song by any means, but it is catchy and an earworm.

'See Me In The Mirror' sounds like Alice is singing to you in your nightmares. It has an eerie, haunted house-style quality. The musical backing is subdued with a prominent drum machine and some keyboards. Alice provides his own harmony vocals, singing it really well. It's a slight piece but has a strangeness to it that pulls you back from time to time. You can hear elements of *Dada* in this one.

'Be Chrool To Your Scuel' (from Twisted Sister's Come Out And Play, 9 November 1985)

Any song with complaints about school makes you think of Alice, and it was a no-brainer for self-confessed fan Dee Snider to ask him to share the microphone. The other VIP guests on the song are Billy Joel (piano), Clarence Clemons (saxophone) and Brian Setzer (guitar). It's pretty much a straight mid-tempo rocker with '50s-style rock 'n' roll tropes. The main positive from the song is that it meant Alice was on his way back. He acquits himself well, with a delivery that's akin to his 1970s peaks. The future suddenly looked bright for 'the Coop".

1986 – Constrictor

Constrictor (MCA)
Personnel:
Alice Cooper: vocals
Kane Roberts: guitar, bass, keyboards, drums, backing vocals
Donnie Kisselbach: bass
Kip Winger: bass, backing vocals
David Rosenberg: SP-12 drum programming on 'Simple Disobedience' and 'Give It Up'
With:
Beau Hill: backing vocals
Paul Delph: keyboards, backing vocals on 'He's Back'
Tom Kelly: backing vocals on 'He's Back'
Produced at Atlantic Studios, New York and Amigo Studios, Los Angeles, January -February 1986 by Beau Hill and Michael Wagener (except 'He's Back', Summer 1986 at Amigo, produced by Michael Wagener)
Release date: 22 September 1986
Highest chart places: UK: 8, USA: 23
Running time: 37:07

Alice and family relocated back to Phoenix in the early months of '86. It was time to get down to business with Kane, whose world had changed so dramatically: 'Suddenly, I have a house in California. I stayed in Maui for three months to work with Alice writing material for the Constrictor record. We would go to these little home studios all over Maui and record these things. 'Hard Rock Summer' was definitely one of the first, also 'Life And Death Of The Party'. That was the song where Alice and I felt we had got into a different mould. We bonded more writing-wise. My influence was always to get a little heavier, like with 'The World Needs Guts' or 'Teenage Frankenstein' – Alice loved it. Whatever genre or situation he is in, he always delivers. I got in the flow and stepped into the jet stream and then it was kind of non-stop till '88'.

Prior to entering a recording studio, Alice wanted to play the songs in with a band, and he knew just the right rhythm section to work with – former fellow Alice Cooper Group members Dennis Dunaway and Neal Smith. Neal recalls that: 'We, Alice, Kane, Dennis and I, worked, wrote and rehearsed at the studio in my house in Connecticut for two weeks'. It's mouth-watering to think of the possibilities that were there, but

Neal says that 'It was always crystal clear that drums and bass on the *Constrictor* album would be synthesised in the studio'. That decision to use Simmons electronic drums was the decision of producer Beau Hill. Despite that, Alice still had his own ideas, says Smith. 'He wanted to work on the arrangements with a live band. Since we hadn't seen each other or played together in ten years, Dennis and I were very much up for it!'

For Kane, it was, 'One of the big moments for me. We hung out; we went to dinner. We played a little bit. I was brand new and freaked out that those guys were there. Neal and Dennis have always been icons. Dennis held the bass somewhere down near his knees. Nobody did that, and it was just like this tall guy kind of lumbering around. Neal was the consummate rock star drummer with the gold Bentley and the big high-heeled boots and everything. It was exciting to play with them. I was still a newbie, but I thought it sounded killer! We would have looked great as well; both guys are iconic true rock stars!' Kane believed there was a possibility of the sessions leading to a four-piece band: 'That's what I thought. I think it was some sort of experiment and I knew we were moving to different types of musicians. No judgement was made, we played great and nobody said anything else to me'.

Kane wasn't the only one wondering if there was a possibility of the foursome being a band. Dennis observes that: 'Nothing was really said other than Alice said, 'hey let's get together'. So what else were we supposed to think when we're working up songs for the album with Alice and Kane. I'm not sure why it didn't solidify; we had a lot of fun and it looked like it was gonna happen. Kane was great. The problem for me was I had the flu, I was telling Alice, 'I don't even wanna be in the same room as you guys because you might get it'. I had a high fever going and I just felt really bad, but I could still play! We did a song that I wrote called 'The Wild Ones'. It was kind of like transferring Marlon Brando and the motorcycle gang to a band showing up and taking over a town. We did a couple of songs that ended up on Alice's album. In hindsight, I kind of blamed my condition because I was so sick and not my perky grab-the-bull-by-the-horns self in the studio. That may have been a factor, but I think the main factor is that Neal and I don't play metal, but that's what the songs ended up as. They ended up getting a metal treatment, whereas Neal and I gave them a swing treatment which is what is in all of the Alice Cooper material – original band. But that's me maybe overthinking it'.

Neal remains full of enthusiasm: 'Over that two-week period, we rehearsed nine songs as a trio with a lead singer like The Who, something I had always wanted to do. With Kane, Dennis and me, it was a killer three-piece band. I still have the four-track recording on cassette of all nine songs we worked on – 'Simple Disobedience', 'Guess Who's Coming To Kill You?', 'You Name It, We Hate It', 'Tyrianhicyde' (probably a misnamed 'Tyrannicide'), 'Nature Of The Beast', 'Harmonious Death Maze', 'The Wild Ones', 'The World Needs Guts', 'All Hell Is Breaking Loose'.

Of the nine he listed, seven have not appeared anywhere since. Kane was still unsure about the decision to use synthesised drums, and after having played with Neal Smith, you can understand why! He says, 'My first choice on *Constrictor* was to have Anton Fig play drums', which would have been a terrific decision. The legendary Anton Fig would have really got things moving in the sterile rhythm tracks.

Sessions for *Constrictor* (working title *Awake For The Snake*) started in New York in January 1986, with Beau Hill initially producing. Alice told *Faces* (December 1986) that *Constrictor* was 'The heaviest album I have ever done as far as sound-wise. Lyrically it's pretty heavy, too. Some of the stronger cuts on the album are 'The World Needs Guts', and 'Teenage Frankenstein'. Lyrically everything is very Cooper-esque. It's got a lot of a black sense of humour to it'.

It was good to see Alice back and in better health, but *Constrictor* is not without flaws. Yes, there is black humour; yes, it is 'heavy', but one of the things that always made an Alice album great was the diversity of the material. On *Constrictor,* much of the material is in a similar vein with little light and shade. There's a distinct feeling of dumbing down, starting with the comic book sleeve. It's a cartoony garish image that actually does fit the music well. The back cover legs are those of Brian Nelson, who did so much for our hero.

On the album itself, the tracks that stand out are those that provide something more involving. The metal tracks that dominate do have something going for them in several cases, but there is a similarity to them that gets dull.

The synth-based rhythm tracks proved to be something that they just couldn't get right. Donnie Kisselbach was invited in to redo all the bass parts: 'I'd been with Rick Derringer since 1979, so Alice likely made that connection. I'd guess the producer contacted me on Alice's instruction. Kane had played 'guide' bass tracks for the purposes of assembling songs to be sung by Alice. I replaced all the tracks on that record, though some of those bass tracks were possibly re-recorded by Kip Winger. For reasons I never quite understood, the drums were on tape courtesy of the SP-12. The overall production was quite weak, so, at some point, either MCA Records or Alice (or both) was dissatisfied with the progress in this regard. I was recruited to breathe some life into the tracks, which I enjoyed immensely! We sat at the console and Alice (some songs with Kane) asked me, 'Do you wanna hear the bass on playback' meaning the bass that was already there, and also meaning, 'Do you wanna use it as a guide to learn the song?' So I'd ask, 'Do you like any of it?' and he'd say: 'No, it doesn't work for the song, I'm looking for something stronger, more balls' (or heavier, or rockier, or more of a hook, or whatever was on his mind at the time). So I'd say, 'OK, if there's no reason to keep it, just wipe it as we go; I don't need to hear it'. So we just went down the list of tracks he had on tape and did it with each one. Alice and Kane worked with me when nailing the best approach for a given section. All I did was put it on tape. I did not play on 'The Man Behind the Mask'. I think it has keyboard bass on it. I never asked who played on what tracks because it had nothing to do with me; I was there simply to replace it. I blew through the entire record in a day and a half and they were thrilled'.

The 'breath of life' Donnie referred to didn't include replacing those synth drums. Kane says that 'David Rosenberg is playing a drum machine on 'Simple Disobedience' and 'Give It Up''. That means the other tracks must be programmed by Kane. Kisselbach clarifies that: 'Rosenberg was the SP-12 programmer, not the drummer. It's important to remember the 1980s as a time when technology became a prominent tool for certain producers in the rock realm. The production on this particular project was seen by some as sterile, cold, and lifeless due to the unnecessary overuse of Emulator samples. There were Emulator bass tracks we recorded over while I was there'.

Beau Hill, at least, still wasn't happy, so he called in Kip Winger. Winger recalls, 'I'd been friends with Beau since I was 16. He called me one day and said, 'We need a bass player for Alice Cooper songs, so grab your bass and get up here'. I went up to Atlantic and they were putting the record together, but it was just Alice and Kane. They recorded it all to a click track with the drum machine. There was this hotshot drum machine guy named David Rosenberg. David had the latest, greatest emulator, and he was a really good programmer; very creative. Beau just loved it because he hated recording organic drums. It was much easier to have a direct signal of his drum samples. But it feels different for a bass player playing with a drum machine because you don't have the emotion of locking in with a drummer or playing with them, even if you're cutting into the track. Having said that, it drives me nuts if the shit's not in time. I want a drummer that can play like a drum machine and give it a human feel; that's Ken Mary! I was a pretty good bass player. I played a BC Rich Mockingbird; that was the bass I had. They gave me a tape of the songs and I learned them. I think I played on 'Teenage Frankenstein', 'Thrill My Gorilla', 'Give It Up' and maybe 'Crawlin'.' Kane saw a lot of good qualities in Kip and says, 'We became great friends. He's a fantastic musician'.

There were changes and additions made all the way through till June. Kip felt things didn't turn out as well as they could have done: 'I have to say I was disappointed in the outcome of the album. It started with Beau Hill but it turned into something else with Michael Wagener and I felt like a lot of corners were cut in the production of the songs. They were originally way more elegant and cool. Beau was producing Alice Cooper and he had another gig to do with Fiona, so he says, 'Hey Alice, I got to go and I'll let my engineer Stephen Benben mix the record. He'll be great'. Alice was like, 'Who is this fucking asshole?' So he got Michael Wagener to finish it'.

With Wagener now in the production seat, he also felt changes were needed. Kane explains that, 'We went from Beau Hill's world into Michael Wagener's world. The drums that were there that we recorded with Beau Hill were just inappropriate for the music. To me, they were just a little too jazzy or progressive. Alice and I felt the simplicity of the songs was what would sell them and the sounds were really good. So I did more programming (of the drums)'.

However, Kip feels they got it wrong: 'When they redid the drums with a drum machine with Mike Wagener, they did a much worse job. The original drums that David programmed were way cooler'.

Inevitably changing the drum programming on most of the songs created new problems. Kane continues: 'Michael said: 'Well, the drums are different now, so we have to change the bass'. There were no bass players around and we didn't really have a band, so I played some bass on it. So that was me trying to get things done because we had already spent a couple of months on the record'.

The offer of a song in the film *Friday The 13ᵗʰ* led to the late recording and addition to the album of 'He's Back', which resulted in a video shoot in July on the movie set.

Kip's final words on *Constrictor* are: 'By the way, they spelled my name wrong on the record (Wringer). That was my entree into the big time, and oh God, that hurt!' Kane's summary of the album is that '*Constrictor* is two minds finding themselves, working together'.

'Teenage Frankenstein' (Cooper/ Roberts)
Another paean to the teenager who just doesn't fit in with his peer group. *Life And Crimes* specifically only credits three performers on the song – Alice, Kane and Kip – with the latter only on backing vocals. Kane says it was fun to put together: 'When Alice wrote those lyrics, he was laughing the whole time; we were having a blast writing it'.

It opens with a thunderstorm which could have been expanded on more to build up the return of Alice – a doomy keyboard piece or voice-over, perhaps? But it's cut short, effectively enough, by Kane's mighty riff, and he builds on that with shredded guitar squeals. All good stuff and setting out the stall that this is going to be a metal album. The big build-up leaves you waiting eagerly for Alice, but he's a little underwhelming. There is a throatiness there and the mid-range soup in the production leaves any dynamics and expression in his voice sounding thin. Kip's backing vocals mask this on the choruses, adding extra range and higher notes.

It's a good song but nothing special. It was released as a single and a video was filmed for it.

'Give It Up' (Cooper/ Roberts)
The fizzing riffs herald a bright, almost poppy track. Alice is in better voice on this one, with the mid-ranges sounding less cluttered than on 'Frankenstein'. It's another fist-pumping chorus with great backing vocals.

There's a dumb kind of vibe to the tune with the all too brief stand-out section coming at 2:20 – 'Just when you got it made, and all the bills are paid' – with Alice changing the key and Kane playing nice complementary guitar. The solo that follows is good, and credit to Kane for keeping a tight rein on all his solos. None of them outstays their welcome, and neither does this average track.

'Thrill My Gorilla' (Cooper/ Roberts)

Kane recalls that 'Alice and I were sitting in the studio in New York and we started getting humorous with the lyrics. I said, 'Where were you when monkey turned to man?', and he came back with, 'Where were you when the monkey hit the fan?' We were laughing so hard; we just decided to record the song'.

It's good to know Alice and Kane were enjoying themselves, and their fun does come over in the song. There's a nagging persistence to the goofy choruses that is an earworm, and they pile them into a Desmond Child level! The call-and-response backing vocals are a really good part of this. However, this is still much more fast food than gourmet meal.

'Life And Death Of The Party' (Cooper/ Roberts)

This song is easily one of the best on the album. The different textures and flavours that open the track are a relief. Kane's big opening guitar parts set things up beautifully for a nuanced thoughtful interlude with terrific interwoven guitars. Vocally, Alice is back on 'Frankenstein' levels, with his voice sitting a little low in the mix. That being said, it's still his best performance yet on the record, with some of those old Cooper touches. His intro lines are vintage Alice and one of the highlights.

This is a well-constructed song, with the only minor blemish being Kane's solo which doesn't fit the tone of the piece. One trivia note is that the title is 'wrong' because Alice always sings 'The life and THE death' on every chorus.

'Simple Disobedience' (Cooper/ Roberts)

It starts off with those programmed drums at their most dominant and then a passable stomping riff, but your ears prick up with Alice's vocal. The way he sings between the riffs is catchy and appealing, pushing his vocal out front.

The gang-style chorus is rather Kiss-like, and it's down to the verses to give what pleasure there is. The guitar solo grates, but there's a line in the verse after it that pops out, 'Take your laser microscope and try to find an answer, no antidote or drug to cure our special strain of cancer'. It faintly suggested that Alice still had something a little more cerebral in his writing that he could bring out when he wanted.

Kane adds 'It was written for the *Magnificent Seven* movie with Def Leppard. That's the one song that survived from that writing era'.

'The World Needs Guts' (Cooper/ Roberts)
This song is all about standing up against an aggressor. Alice explained to *Concert Shots* (November 1987) that: 'I think we wrote it just when we were about to bomb Libya and the French wouldn't let us fly over France. They were our allies. I was going: 'Hey, come on. It's time to kick the bully's ass, and you guys are wimping out'. I mean, they made us fly all the way around two countries to get there. It kinda pissed me off. Why are they being such wimps about it? So I just said, 'The World Needs Guts'. Then after a while, I thought about it and I thought, well, it also means you can't let the bully down the street push you around either. You can't walk around the extra block because you have to pass the bully on the street. Sometimes you gotta stand up and kick his ass'.

Kane's slide down the strings and trilling opening notes make way for a gritty riff, with the synthesised drums sounding unfortunately obvious. It was a live mainstay of the tour set, and Ken Mary, in particular, gave the song the boost it needed. Lyrically it's as basic as most of the album, but the chorus hook works well enough. The bridge section – 'Hey, hey, what's in your eyes' – adds some diversity and Kane gets off one of his best solos on the album immediately after it. Frustratingly It sounds like he was faded out on the outro as he pulls off a second solo.

This is good, but the live version was much better.

'Trick Bag' (Cooper/ Roberts/ Wagener)
Heavy synths and clattering (synth) percussion give this one a more electronic vibe. When Kane's guitar comes in, there's a more cinematic, expansive feel, which is also picked up in Alice's vocals. This is due to the music being the original tune for 'He's Back', and thus written with the intention for it to sound cinematic.

Here, accompanied by a new set of lyrics, it sounds better than it did when it was to be 'He's Back'. It's not that the lyrics and song are particularly great, but there is more of a sense of purpose, intent and drive here. It shares one problem in common with 'He's Back', in that the choruses don't hit home as well as the verses.

'Crawlin'' (Cooper/ Roberts)
The chugging intro guitar riff is livened up by sparkling keyboards that make for a nicely different texture. Once Alice comes in, though, it's all a bit the same as has gone before. The keyboard highlights are used on the lines leading into the chorus and it sounds promising enough, but

the chorus itself misses the mark. Additionally, the vocals are too low in the mix and it's not a great vocal anyway. However, there is one part that pricks up your ears at 2:09, when Alice intones, 'Come on baby, slither on over here'. Right there, you get some vintage Alice for a few seconds. Overall though, this is one that should have been replaced.

'The Great American Success Story' (Cooper/ Roberts/ Hill)

Kane: 'That one we wrote for the Rodney Dangerfield movie, *Back to School*, and we recorded it with Beau Hill'. It didn't make the movie or the soundtrack, but it is still the other great track on the album. It has a good feel to it and a strong chorus. The lyrics aren't much to get excited about, but there are one or two nods to Alice's way with words. He employs a similar device to one he used on *Dada*'s 'I Love America', when he avoids an obvious rhyme. This time it's 'He thinks about his teacher in his literary class. He's staring at her legs, but he's dreaming 'bout her face'.

The lift from the backing vocals is a big plus, pushing those choruses home. It makes for a very catchy song that, from the credits, must owe a lot to Beau Hill's input. Although the overall sound is more lightweight than most of the record it has a diversity and melody that is refreshing. It's one of the best songs on the album.

'He's Back (The Man Behind The Mask)' (Cooper/ Roberts/ Tom Kelly)

Kane explains 'It was written for *Friday the 13th*, Alice and I wrote a very heavy song, but the record company said we need something that will get the P1 stations, more of like a melodic pop kind of a sound. So they hired the guy that wrote 'Like A Virgin' and we were sitting there writing with him. He was a cool guy, very talented, so we came up with that song. We recorded it, and Frank Mancuso (*Friday the 13th* Producer) came in to hear it. He was tapping his foot but he goes, 'Kane, is this ever gonna rock?' And I went, 'No'. He still used it, but he was very crestfallen. But it came out great and it did very well in certain places. Alice and I were pleased with the song'.

It sounds very different to the rest of the album because of the input from Tom Kelly on the songwriting and his performance on the song with Paul Delph. The one-off configuration that recorded the song was Alice, Kane (guitar, keyboards, backing vocals), Tom Kelly (bass, drums, backing vocals) and Paul Delph (keyboards, backing vocals).

Kelly was known for co-writing many rock/pop hit songs, and you can hear echoes particularly of 'Like A Virgin' in his synth refrain on 'He's Back'. The highly poppy tune sits at odds stylistically, with it being the main song for *Friday the 13ᵗʰ Part VI*. The original tune, as used for 'Trick Bag', was more in keeping, albeit unlikely to sell well as a single.

Musically it's basic. Alice never really seems to get to grips with the delivery either and it's all set up for a chorus that falls well short of the mark. Paul Delph carries most of the tune on his bass synth, along with some utterly dull synth drums. The best parts are Kane's tasteful and reflective solo, with a bridge section that has a pulse to it – 'Oh, if you see him coming, run as fast as you can'. It's all too brief, though and we fade out on more of the limited arrangement.

The edited single (movie) mix of the song is featured on *Life And Crimes* and is far superior to the album version. It has more backing ambience with the mix of the synths and keyboards blended better. There's a better background wash on the chorus, too, with the vocals mixed better. The less up-front mix works well, giving a sense that there is more going on in the arrangement than there actually is.

Related recordings
'Hard Rock Summer' (Cooper/ Roberts)
Also known as 'Summer In The USA'. This was one of the earliest songs written by Alice and Kane and was used in *Friday the 13ᵗʰ Part VI*. It didn't make the cut for *Constrictor* but could easily have done so. Kane handles all instruments, with Alice sounding more like the Alice of old than he does on most of *Constrictor*! The verses are really well done and the way he carries the melody is vintage Alice, with only the rather puny chorus letting it down.

It was recorded at Amigo Studios with Michael Wagener putting a little gloss on it. It was first released on *Life And Crimes*.

'He's Back (demo)' (Cooper/ Roberts)
This demo of the song has more bite than the final version used on the album and in *Friday the 13ᵗʰ Part VI*. Again it's just Alice and Kane involved, recorded at Amigo Studios with Michael Wagener.

The big attraction here is the backing track. It is different to the final version, being the one they used on the album for 'Trick Bag'. There's some nice chattering rhythm guitar lines behind Kane's wall of riffs and, all in all; this is a far more successful spin on the movie theme, save for those awful synth drums again. The chorus backing vocals are less effective too, but on the other hand, Alice is generally better throughout on this demo. Hear it on *Life And Crimes*.

Outtakes
'Don't Blame It On Me' (Cooper/ Roberts)
Kane: 'It was written in Mauai. That was one of the very first we worked on and we were just trying to come up with melodies. I remember one of the concerns on that song was there was a flow from verse to chorus'. This has not been released.

'Full Pull' (Cooper/ Roberts)
From this era comes a song that appeared on Kane Roberts' eponymous debut solo album in 1987. It's better than a lot on *Constrictor* and would have given that album another big gang chorus song.

'Nobody Move' (Cooper/ Beau Hill)
This was recorded for *Constrictor* and was even on a test pressing. It was removed from the running order, possibly to make way for the late-comer 'He's Back'.

Two other outtakes are known to exist, but no information on them has come to light:
'Drain The Vein' (Cooper/ Roberts) and 'If You Don't Like It' (Cooper/ Roberts)

Prince Of Darkness (film, 1987)
John Carpenter's film was shooting over the summer months of 1987 and Alice and Kane secured an invitation to meet him and watch the filming. Alice told *Kerrang* (October 1987) about the unexpected opportunity: 'John Carpenter said, 'Why don't you stand in as one of those bag-people. It'll be really funny because it'll be a really fast pan, so people will go, 'Was that really Alice Cooper and Kane Roberts?' I was totally garbaged out and Carpenter said I looked so good that he wanted to develop the character some more. They had this doctor *(played by Thom Bray)*, who they needed to get rid of, but they didn't have his death planned out. So now he walks out into this alley, seeing all these bag-people. He turns around, and I'm standing there with this bicycle without a front wheel and handlebars. He bumps into me so I push this

bike through him and it comes out the back. Then he rolls over and he's balancing on this frame and stuff starts coming out of his mouth; it's great!' The idea was obviously taken from Franz Harary's stunt, which was used in the *The Nightmare Returns* tour with the photographer.

The appearance in the film inspired Alice and Kane to come up with 'Prince Of Darkness', to be added to *Raise Your Fist And Yell*.

The Nightmare Returns Tour
20 October 1986 (Santa Barbara, California) to 30 August 1987 (Reading Festival, England)

Setlist: 'Welcome To My Nightmare', 'Billion Dollar Babies', 'No More Mister Nice Guy', 'Be My Lover', 'I'm Eighteen', 'The World Needs Guts', 'Give It Up', 'Cold Ethyl', 'Only Women Bleed', 'Go To Hell', 'Ballad Of Dwight Fry', 'Teenage Frankenstein', 'Sick Things', 'I Love The Dead', 'School's Out', 'Elected', 'Under My Wheels'
(A snippet of 'Years Ago' was played before 'No More Mr Nice Guy' and 'Be My Lover')
Musicians: Kane Roberts (lead guitar, vocals), Arti Funaro aka Devlin 7 (guitar), Paul Taylor aka Paul Horrors (keyboards, guitar, vocals), Kip Winger (bass, vocals), Ken Mary (drums)
Stage performers: Linda Albertano, Trace Devai (also backing vocals), Sylvia Dohi (also Dwight Fry's daughter vocal), Karen Russell (replaced Dohi on 9 January)

Kane Roberts was the musical director, with the responsibility to pick the band members: 'I had to get the right musicians who would be able to handle the arrangements. I knew that there wasn't just performing the songs but also the massive scope of the Alice Cooper show. So whoever I was playing with had to speak the same language'.

Quite when the second guitarist was appointed is hazy, but *Kerrang* reported in October 1986 that Kane and Randy Piper (from WASP) were on guitars for the tour with the other band positions still unknown, implying that Piper was one of the first to get the gig. Kane was initially hopeful: 'I thought Randy Piper might be a good addition'.

Kane and Alice's first thoughts for a bass player had been Donnie Kisselbach. They were knocked out by his prowess and speed at getting the parts down for *Constrictor*, so they made him an offer: 'Alice asked me to join the band for the tour, asking me to bring along a drummer I'd wanna work with. Alice had no drummer on this record, so he was wanting to kick-start a new group with Kane, me and a drummer of my choice. I told him we could talk about it tomorrow when we meet at the studio again, but he said, 'But you're all done; ya nailed it'. 'No, no', I replied, 'We need to listen back to everything tomorrow with fresh ears and either it sounds exactly right, or I can fix what needs to be fixed and then we're done'. By that next session, I knew I couldn't leave the country to tour with them since I had commitments with Johnny Winter and also separately with Rick Derringer. I had a blast working with Alice. Felt like I'd known him all my life'.

With Kisselbach turning down the chance to tour, Kip Winger got the gig. He says, 'Kane was the one who suggested I go on the tour. I'd said to them, if you guys need a bass player, hit me up because I'm ready to go. They called me and I didn't have to audition'.

The drummer was next. 'We auditioned a bunch of drummers', says Kip, 'And then Ken Mary walked in and blew everybody's mind. It was just so clear he had got the gig. He was so much better than everybody else'. Mary vividly remembers the audition process: 'I was playing a gig at the Whisky A Go Go (Los Angeles) with a guitarist named Randy Hansen. Some of Alice's management company were there and saw me playing. They said they thought I was a great player and did I want to come down to audition. I lived in Seattle at the time and I was pretty young, so they said, 'Well, we're not flying anybody down, but if you want to fly down, we'll get an audition spot for you'. They sent seven songs and they were all from the older albums. I think it was like 'Eighteen', 'Go To Hell', 'School's Out' and four others. For the audition, I learned those songs forwards and backwards, but we only jammed on a couple of the songs. Then we jammed on the newer arrangements and some of the new songs that were gonna be played on the tour. There were three days of auditions and I was on day two. I remember Kane Roberts telling me at the end of the audition, 'I can't imagine someone coming in here and doing better than that, but you know we have to go through another day of auditions still. I'd love to tell you you got the gig, but I can't say that yet'. I think the assessment was basically made on 'how does this energy work' and 'Is there a good chemistry between the players?' Mary adds that 'Alice was not at the auditions'.

Paul Taylor was the next musician to be signed up. 'He came in and I think he was the first keyboard player we auditioned', says Kip. Taylor was born Paul Horowitz but says that 'I changed my name just for music stuff because everyone was spelling it wrong'. His musical break came playing with Aldo Nova, and his joining Alice came completely out of the blue: 'I was the only one auditioned for the tour. I got a call from this girl, Sharon Levene, who said, 'We've been looking for you. We need a keyboards/guitar player who can also sing for Alice Cooper. Are you interested?' I said, 'Wow yeah!' She said, 'Can you be in LA in a day or so?' I got there early and Alice showed up. He came walking up to me saying, 'Hey, are you the keyboard player for the audition?' I said yeah and he said, 'Does your name start with a K?' I said no and he says, 'OK you've got the gig'. I said 'why?' He said, 'I've got a Kane, a Kip and a Ken; I don't want any more Ks!' I said, 'OK, I'm Paul'. We got in there and he said, 'Do you know 'Eighteen'?' I said yeah. We got halfway through the song and he stopped and said, 'You can sing back-ups, right?' I said yeah so he said, 'You got the gig; this stuff's not rocket science'. Taylor elaborates, 'I played guitar when there were no keyboards. I did a fair amount of guitar'.

In the meantime, concerns were voiced over Randy Piper's suitability. 'Musically Randy was in just a different little space', says Mary, while Kane discretely explains that, 'It didn't quite mesh in terms of style. He was a great player, though; it wasn't one of those. So I got Arti to come'.

Time was short by now, but Arti Funaro wasn't one to panic: 'As usual, I was not the first choice for a gig', he drolly observes. 'Doesn't play well with others', was my reputation. I have very little patience. I came into an air of mild desperation. Apparently, just a few weeks before the tour, Randy showed some difficulty playing a simple chord. As usual, the gig was panicked to find someone to learn and play the whole show perfectly with little time. That is who I am. That is what I always do. I learned the whole show in about three days. Sighs of relief all around'.

Two of the band changed their names for the tour. Arti adopted the mysterious pseudonym of Devlin 7: 'Kane gave me the name Devlin 7 many years before the whole Alice thing. The name suited my antisocial behaviour and cynical outlook on life in general. I could get away with being caustic, annoying, offensive, insulting, disgusting and borderline sociopathic just by doing it in the guise of a character'. Paul Taylor was named Paul Horrors by Alice. 'That was Alice's funny joke', he says. 'He is very witty'.

The show was set to be a big production with new effects and routines, as well as the return of the guillotine. As part of the step-up in production values, three performers were recruited for the tour, with Sheryl Cooper taking time out from the stage for the first time.

Trace Devai recalls that: 'Greg Smith (casting director) called me to do Alice Cooper. He said they needed somebody really thin and I was *really* thin. So I didn't really audition for it; they just gave me the gig, which was doing illusions. I had to be small to fit inside these special things to look like there was nothing in there, I was teenage Frankenstein!'

The imposing Linda Albertano was spotted by Alice's production manager Joe Gannon: 'He said it was going to be a post-apocalyptic world. So I put on a costume, long rags and such, and went down to the office to do a three-minute mime, understanding that the show was going to open with this post-apocalyptic performance. I was completely wrong. Joe called Alice in and I did it again for him. Alice said, 'I'm not interested in any of this artsy fartsy crap'. But they asked me to be the executioner and the evil nurse. They let me participate in the design of the costumes. We had a bra with two very elongated pointed metallic breasts. I also had a metallic low-slung belt with sabre tooth tiger teeth hanging from it. Then there was a cape and I decided I should wear a bald head wig. They let me go ahead with that'.

Sylvia Dohi recalls 'I got the gig from an open audition. There was one callback and then I was hired. Alice was there for the callback and it was really cool to meet him. I heard that I was hired because Alice said I reminded him of a female version of himself, which I still cherish as a great compliment! He had a nickname for me, 'Sly', which I still love to this day'.

Rehearsals took place for around five weeks in late summer 1986 in Los Angeles on a soundstage, possibly on the Fox studio lot. The thinking was for it to be a refresher course in 'old' Alice alongside material from *Constrictor*. Deciding the balance between old and new songs wasn't easy, and choosing the older songs was even more difficult. 'There's no way Alice Cooper could do a show without 'Eighteen', 'Be My Lover', 'School's Out', 'Only Women Bleed' and 'Welcome To My Nightmare', Alice told *Aardschok* (January 1987). '(But) that still leaves us plenty of room to do five songs off the new record on this tour'. Even five proved a stretch as the show needed the visual high points provided by the likes of 'Dwight Fry' and 'I Love The Dead', so the five new songs were reduced to three. Alice recalled to *Concert Shots* (November 1987) that they had thought that 'Man Behind the Mask', 'Thrill My Gorilla', and 'Life and Death of the Party' were going to work, but they didn't'.

The truth is that the quality of the old material remains immense, and that, plus the strength of the visuals, would have been more than enough to keep everyone happy. Alice's claim that they would have used more *Constrictor* material *if* it had worked live, would have been at the expense of the classics, and in truth, *Constrictor* was no *Trash*-style major album.

Mary says the setlist was the immediate priority: 'This was his big comeback tour and there were so many classics that had to be put in there, so that was the first order of business. The second was what new songs, while the third was how do you turn it into a show. Joe Gannon was involved in putting the shows together. Sometimes he would have ideas that we liked thinking they would go very well, and other times there would be ideas that we didn't. But he would come up with a hundred ideas; maybe twenty were great and eighty weren't great, but you still had a lot of great ideas to sift through and choose from. Kane was the musical director, so he assembled the music, then Joe, Alice and Shep made sure that the show as a whole was everything that it needed to be'.

As part of getting things right, Taylor says, 'Alice would cut out part of a song to make the show work. So when we were working a song out, if something was too long and the monsters had to get across or something, he would go, 'Make it four bars less' or whatever. Kane would work with Alice and the band. He put in the lion's share of the work. He was responsible for getting everything produced. We would just go in saying, 'What have we got to do?'

Mary enjoyed settling in with the band: 'When you're in Alice's band, there is a certain amount of pressure on you to be more of whatever it is. When I came in, I was doing stick twirling and tossing and all that stuff. Shep pulled me aside, saying, 'What else can you do?' You know, like, can you light your hair on fire? What else can we put into the show!'

The guillotine had not been seen for a long time and had never been seen at all in Europe. To extend the visual feast, magician Franz Harary was brought on board to come up with other illusions as well as sharpen up the guillotine stunt. Harary had impressed Alice with his work for The Jacksons, Michael Jackson and Styx. But the first contact came from Harary: 'I knew and liked some of his music, *Welcome To My Nightmare* particularly. I pursued him by tracking down his manager because I knew that he had done magic in the past. Most people want a copy of the last idea I worked on, but Alice is one of the few who has said, 'Hey, I have this idea'. The illusions were driven by the method and that often dictates the look. Alice is an actor playing a character, so what

I did for Alice was to basically use the raw effect without the fanfare. The ideas were pretty much mine and then Alice put his spin on it. It was us playing creative ping-pong. He was an experienced artist, used to working with other professionals – it wasn't a power trip for him like it is with some'.

Alice told *Metal Hammer* in December 1986 that: 'It took a lot of time to work out some of the special effects. The guillotine, this time, is a lot more dangerous than it was before. It's a forty-pound blade and in order to make it a lot more effective, we have to make it a little more dangerous'. Harary remembers, 'Kind of cleaning the guillotine up. It had got kind of sloppy. I restaged it a little bit because it just looked like they had gotten bored of it'. The stunt proved hard for Albertano (the executioner) to get her head round: 'It was a very heavy blade and he was rehearsing it with one of the stagehands. The issue was if the blade dropped or his timing was off, he would have been decapitated. As I was watching it, I was feeling butterflies inside; I was very nervous. Finally, I got my chance to rehearse it, the matter of timing, counting out the beats and pulling the cord at exactly the right moment'.

Harary came up with two other big stunts for the show: 'We did a thing where he assembled a robot. It came to life and then he knocked the robot apart. Then there was the thing with the microphone stand. A cameraman comes up onstage, he has a one-on-one with Alice and Alice takes a microphone stand, pushing it through him. The original idea was that it would pierce the cameraman, blood would go everywhere and the cameraman would kind of stumble off. But we were having a problem with the rig, getting the microphone stand to lock into the rig the cameraman was wearing. Alice realised that he could make it look like he had broken off the microphone stand, which was technically easier to do, and made it look grosser. The mic stand contracted into itself, hooking up to a harness. Then the back harness had a telescoping barrel that would come out. Very low-tech but effective. There were canisters under each armpit from which the fake blood would come out when he squeezed. Having it be a cameraman helped because he would be carrying equipment, so it helped conceal everything. We also did a lot of hand props too'. Harary stayed with the tour for the first two weeks to make sure his effects and props were working properly as well as being handled correctly.

Mary recalls, 'The final night of dress rehearsals, we actually invited celebrities in. I remember Weird Al was there. There were huge numbers of famous people there, but the one guy I remember was him. I remember going to Kip, 'Weird Al's right there man!'

Alice's first live show after four years away was in Santa Barbara on 20 October with Guns 'N' Roses. The tour was the first Alice had done as a teetotaller and the first when he decided to 'become Alice' only when performing. Alice explained to *Metal Hammer* (December 1986) that: 'There's a totally psyching into being Alice. It's all mental. I don't go into the dressing rooms, I always dress in the bus. I get the Alice drag on and I get the Alice make up on. I'm totally alone until I go on but as soon as I hit the stage, then I become Alice'.

Mary observes that: 'This was a very important tour for Alice. Shep wasn't sure it was gonna be successful. Nobody really knew if it was going to do well, but the idea was to put something together that was very powerful, very energetic, very entertaining'. He adds that: 'I was well prepared because I had been touring with Randy Hansen. But Kane had been working in the studio with Alice for two years and Kip had been in the studio for three or four years too, so I think the whole band was a little bit nervous'.

One decision that bothered long-term fans was the freshening up of the classic songs. In particular, allowing Kane to change the guitar solos to something more metallic. Alice was adamant that this was the right way to go. He explained to *Creem* (March 1988): 'We took songs like 'Eighteen' and 'No More Mr Nice Guy', and I told the band, 'OK, here's this song. Now take it and play it the way you would play it as if you wrote it last week'. We just kind of updated everything a little. We satisfied everybody, I think, because everybody loves hearing those songs again, but they love hearing them big and tough. There's always a few people that will say, 'I liked that a lot better the other way', and I can understand that, but I don't hear any of the young kids saying that. I'd say 75 per cent of my audience now is pretty much 16 to 23'. Kane praises Alice's openness to change. 'Alice played with a heavy metal band that messed around with his arrangements from the '70s. He was cool with that and just did it'. Taylor adds, 'It evolved a bit once the band got together. They were definitely a different style of song. I like the vibe of the '70s stuff. Alice was like, 'man, let's make this current'. He wanted to update it and sometimes it's fun to take a new approach'.

Mary's view is that: 'An attempt was made to put a fresh coat of paint on them, so to speak. That was nothing new, Alice has done that many times in his career; you look at him in the early '80s when he went in an almost new-wave direction. Kane was obviously a metal guitar player, and I think his instinct was to take Alice in a more metal direction, which for that time period was perfect. Those tours were hugely successful. It was the right call with the right band and energy for that time'.

The freshening up sometimes worked. 'While the likes of 'Be My Lover' or 'Elected' suffered as a result with jarring guitar solos, the opener, 'Welcome To My Nightmare', lost 99% of its jazzy structure and became a simpler blast of metal, yet still retained some charm. There were unexpected keyboard delights in 'Dwight Fry' and 'Sick Things' where Taylor's work made a difference that was appropriate. His keyboards on 'Dwight Fry' are empathic, capturing the tone of the piece perfectly, while 'Sick Things' worked with drum pad triggers on the intro and some stellar keyboards.

Not all of the band were convinced about the rejuvenation of the classics. Kip wasn't happy: 'Honestly? I was disappointed at the way we handled the early material because I felt it was biblical. The original band and those records were unbelievable. Dennis Dunaway was one of my biggest influences. I was 12 when *Billion Dollar Babies* came out and I learned every part on that album. As the bass player, I tried to stick very true to the original stuff. I wanted to play Dennis's parts in honour of Dennis. You should never fuck with that stuff at all. That's what people want to hear. Kane didn't give a shit about that; he was like let's update it and make it a metal thing. To me, those songs were sacred. I felt like the tempos weren't right – it was all just too sloppy. It was a really good band, capable of basically anything, but I felt we could have handled some of the material with a lot more grace'.

Funaro was easy either way: 'I had no preference. I was not really familiar with Alice's work except for 'School's Out' and 'Eighteen'. I am a bluesman and a classical violinist who can play most anything else. Gotta eat, right?'

Two hometown shows in Detroit came quickly on the schedule. Mary was soon adding huge enthusiasm to his astonishing ability, but Alice needed a word with him. 'I was very young and playing these coliseums for the first time in my life. As the show was going on, my drums started getting more and more complicated. I was starting to play more and more fills, so it was sounding like a drum solo going on through the night. Now Alice never really said anything about the music to anybody; he enjoyed what we did and just went and did his job. But he came up to me and he goes, 'Hey Ken, could you maybe, I don't know, pull it back just a little bit?' I thought to myself, 'Oh crap, what am I actually doing?' So I went to Robert Scoville, the sound man, saying, 'Hey can I get a board mix from last night?' I listened to it and there were drums just walking all over everything. I thought that was just the coolest thing because he's Alice Cooper, and he could have been like, 'Hey man, you need to calm down!' Nothing like that, he was just so cool, and he's a legend. He was just so non-aggressive about it. Detroit seemed pretty good, so it must have been in the shows after then that I started to get a little overzealous on the drums because I was having such a good time'.

One thing missing from the shows was two guitarists swapping licks and lead solos, something that had been present to varying degrees on previous Cooper tours. Funaro's perspective on it is that: 'The twin lead approach only works when both guitarists are talented, no jealousy, ego-less, secure and friendly. You also need executives that care more about the music than the image. None of those important elements were present. It was very tough. I was pissed off a lot. I would imagine how I would have approached a solo or a groove on this or that. I would have approached the whole thing differently, musically'.

Consequently, it left Funaro handling rhythm guitar (mostly): 'I just tried to stay out of the way, back on my rafter, behind everything. I got to play a character which saved me from death by boredom. I got to play one solo per night (on 'School's Out'). I got more mileage from that solo than a Volkswagen. You could tell who were the real musicians on that stage, and who was there for some other motive. I started each show by myself in the spotlight, and then the band joined in. That was fun'.

Kip gritted his teeth when it came to his bass solo: 'Dude, I'm not a bass solo guy. I didn't want to do one; I'm the rhythm guy. So that freaked me out'.

Of the new songs, 'Teenage Frankenstein' had to be revamped with an extended middle section to fit in with the giant robot assembly. Devai's main role was to operate the Frankenstein monster: 'I would get in there and I would be collecting all this stuff while the show is going on, springs and contraptions and things. Then I had to chase him around and not fall over, even walk up the stairs. There was only one time it nearly messed up. There was an escape hatch that was supposed to slide down and I drop through it. Then Alice pushes the monster and there's nothing in it. But this time the hatch bolts were not connected, so I couldn't get in it and I couldn't slide down. The drum roll's going and Alice is waiting to push the monster. He knows I'm not down yet. It was like the last second, one of those Hollywood moments, and he had to push because there was no way to hold it any longer. They said they could see my head going down really fast. What was really cool though, was when I was down there, I was onstage for the next three songs because I couldn't move. So Alice would come and sing these songs right in front of me every night. A camera couldn't have been closer to him than I was, so I would sit there, watching him perform. I watched him get guillotined every night, too, from the same perspective'.

Dohi appeared in four places in the show: 'I was a post-apocalyptic crawling creature in the opening (along with Devai), the woman who bled in 'Only Women Bleed' and then the whip dancer in 'Go To Hell'. I came back out in my S&M costume and threw giant balloons filled with confetti into the audience for 'Elected'. The attention to detail impressed Sylvia, especially that 'the dummy that Alice pulled out of an onstage prop refrigerator for 'Cold Ethyl' was made to look like me for my appearance in 'Only Women Bleed'.'

Dohi also did the daughter's voice for the intro of 'Dwight Fry' and some backing vocals: 'We had a backstage mic where we added to the repeated background vocals for 'I Love The Dead'. Devai sang on that, too, as well as many other songs: 'I did the backing vocals in my quick-change booth in my costume. I was just back there with a hand-held mic singing 'Schools Out', all of them. If I wasn't onstage, I was singing backstage'.

Funaro recalls an early high point for him: 'I used my Gibson SG for the first week and then our free guitars came in. I used an Ibanez (a black one, I don't remember the model) and a Kramer Voyager with Steve Vai pickups'. 'Arti was such a great guitar player', says Devai. 'I was friends with the sound man, so every night, he would give me the set to listen to the mixes of the shows. Arti's guitars were just so fucking good'.

There was no scope in the show for jamming because, says Funaro, 'It was considered uncool by the bandleader (Kane). The closest we came to that was the idiotic way we wasted time at sound checks. I was instrumental in making them very silly. It was the only relief we had from long bus rides and living out of a suitcase'. It was indeed a long hard schedule of travel/hotel/gig on repeat.

Albertano says the sheer slog of touring was tough at first: 'Joe Gannon told me they were taking the show to China and I would have done anything to go to China. I don't know if there was a real possibility of that. I think that's what he told us to keep us on board because it was a little rocky at the beginning of the tour, stopping in mean little motels.

The better hotels came later'. She recalls the tour bus vividly: 'We lived in relative splendour, furnished with a refrigerator, indoor plumbing, tables, captain's chairs, TVs and video players, plus two ultra-comfy lounges separated by cosy stacked bunk beds'.

Entertainment-wise, Albertano says that 'Constant horror movies were shown, which was cool because there were two sections to the bus and there was a lot of privacy. So they would go to the back section and turn on the TV and enjoy *It's Alive* or whatever else they were watching'. It wasn't all horror, though, as Dohi remembers: 'We were watching the movie *Spinal Tap* on the bus early on in the tour and pulled into a Holiday Inn hotel with a sign that said something like, 'Welcome Elks Club and Alice Cooper', which I thought was hilariously ironic. On one trip, Alice and Kane were making up this hilarious improv' rap song that had me laughing so hard I almost fell out of my bus seat!' 'Oh my God, Kane kept us in stitches', adds Albertano. 'He is so funny; he and Alice had this great patter all the time'.

Taylor also has fond memories of the bus: 'Being in a band with Alice and Kane was so funny. Alice was so much different than I thought. I used to enjoy sitting on the bus and listening to his stories'. Devai also enjoyed it when 'Alice would tell me these great stories. He would always watch karate movies. You know, we were all on the same bus the whole damn time. There was a closet in the bus that only had golf clubs'.

Albertano was taken with Alice's down-to-earth personality on shopping expeditions: 'Alice Cooper is one of the most personable humans on the planet. During the day you arrive at your hotel, you go out and you shop. Alice knows the location of every Chess King (men's clothing store) in America! We went to the Mall Of America in Bloomington, and I would see him just sitting down on a bench talking to a little old lady or a fifteen-year-old kid, just anybody'.

There were times they could all let their hair down. Funaro freely admits there were perks of the gig: 'I had some real adventures with that band. Most of the anecdotes involve non-music types. For example, I did not go after the big-haired blondes that hung around the stage after the show. I *knew* what they had done to get those all-access backstage passes. I went for the female security guards in the sports arenas. They would show up two at a time to my hotel rooms after the show, much to the amazement of others in the organisation, and they always brought goodies'. Taylor adds, 'Alice had one rule – if you were ever with any girl, then you had better make sure they were at least 18. He was clear that this was serious'.

The support bands could be lively too. Albertano says: 'We seemed to tour with bands with big hair. One of them brought a naked groupie decorated with whipped cream into the dressing room on a dessert trolley. As the tour feminist, I felt compelled to pull her aside afterwards and encourage her to form a union with the other groupies. Because the destination on the front of the tour bus read 'Show Us Your Tits', Sylvia, the lovely whip-dancer, and I made bumper-stickers for the back of the bus reading, 'Reveal Testes or Perish''.

Alice would always turn down parties, says Albertano: 'He was on the wagon. So when we were on the elevator after the show and people were inviting him to parties, he'd say, 'No thanks, I've got an embalming to get to'. Also, he would never accept a drink that had been opened by someone else'. What Alice did do for fun was to encourage Kip to perform his party act: 'I used to carry a leather briefcase with symphonic scores; I was always studying so Alice dubbed me 'the briefcase rocker'. I could also be very crazy and I had this thing called the dick dance. I would do any dare in those days. Like I would come down in the lobby naked, Alice would always egg me on'.

Not surprisingly, there were plenty of *Spinal Tap* moments. Devai recounts some favourites: 'In Texas, we stopped to get booze. Everyone had their money and we all got boots as well. I got the same boots that Kip got; you weren't supposed to do that, you know, so I had to hide them from him. He found out and he stole them from my bag; I couldn't believe it. In Las Vegas (at the Thomason Marks Center), some kids stole our luggage out of our bags and we chased them around this hotel; Kip was part of that too. In Cincinnati, we got a phone call at two in the morning, 'Pack your bags; we're leaving; the snake is missing'. That happened in (Kipps) New York, also'.

Albertano recalls, 'We were driving through the Mid-West, rolling across farmland. We saw the names of porno flicks hand-painted on the side of a barn in thick, crooked black letters. Instead of roadside produce, we're offered bushels of flesh. Alice slides open a window and shouts, 'What's this, America? We give you the Farm Aid Concert and you give us *Debbie Does Dallas!*'

Back onstage, it was a perfect comeback for Alice, who was on imperious form, delighting audiences everywhere. If you took away the visual effects, the band would still have come over well because they were a great unit, hungry and eager to make an impact. Whenever Alice was off stage, the band held your attention, 'just killing it', says Mary.

He loved the set, both old and new material: 'Ones I specifically enjoyed playing were 'Welcome To My Nightmare', 'Eighteen', 'School's Out' and 'The World Needs Guts'. 'Teenage Frankenstein' was a fun one, 'Go To Hell' was another great one. I mean, these are all amazing songs'.

The band remain full of admiration (mostly) for each other, and especially Alice. For Mary, 'Every night was awe-inspiring to be onstage with Alice, you'd look up and say, 'heck he's right there, there's Alice!'' Funaro recalls that 'Ken Mary was amazing, a phenomenal drummer. I got to play over his right shoulder every night. He was a machine! Kip was one of the best musicians I had ever worked with. Crazy as a loon but great, diverse and way crazy good on that bass. Paul was like me, just fading into the woodwork, keeping the rhythm solid. He had great patch selections that fitted each song perfectly'.

Kip runs through the band: 'Alice is a fantastic human being. So nice, generous, and very funny. He's one of the guys; there's no ego-tripping. Kane is a special human being, the funniest motherfucker on the planet, with talent in abounds. He's not just a musician; Kane could run a corporation, design the artwork for a Netflix motion picture. He could write a screenplay or become an investment banker. A very talented guy. A really nice guy with no ego and a good guitar player. Arti was fun to be onstage with. I would look across and he would make a funny face. He's a good musician and learned his parts very thoroughly. Ken is an incredible drummer, absolutely amazing. There's good drummers, great drummers, and then there's special musicians like Ken. So is Paul Taylor'.

Kip's career lightbulb moment came one night onstage: 'Bands like Tesla and Megadeth were opening for us. I was there up on my riser going, 'I did that when I was 16, I thought this was over!' So I got together with Ken and Paul Taylor and said, 'Let's put a band together, man, we can do that. I know this great guitar player (Reb Beach)'. That's where the invention of Winger came'.

The *The Nightmare Returns* show followed a similar trajectory to the 1970s shows, moving through the opening rock numbers towards a middle section where Alice's crimes are committed and he pays the price before the glorious resurrection. 'Welcome To My Nightmare' had to be the show opener; it was the perfect set-up for the show. Devai was onstage from the off: 'In the opening number, there were these goblins that come out from behind the trash cans. I was behind the trash can in the centre of the stage, so halfway through I come out and do some weird things'.

A high point for long-term fans was the unexpected inclusion of 'Ballad Of Dwight Fry'. The unfolding drama of the song proved to be as gripping as ever, especially after the death of 'Nurse Ratchet' (as Albertano called herself): 'The nurse was great fun. I loved being so mean. While Alice was trussed in a strait jacket, I'd stomp up behind him armed with a giant syringe. I'd kick him to his knees and plunge the trick needle deep into his neck, drawing out what appeared to be a gallon of blood. Then as I scratched furious notes on a clipboard, Alice slipped from his bindings and threw them around my neck. I gasped and clawed at the air with both hands! As I finally collapsed, there was a colossal roar of approval from the fans! And then I was dragged away, a glow of perfect achievement inwardly warming me'.

Alice's escape during 'Dwight Fry' was made to a soundtrack of eerie keyboards and Mary's triggered drum pads. Taylor also used patches for key effects and enhancements during the show, which included vocals. On 'School's Out', for example, you would hear Alice, the band and Trace Devai singing, but also backed up by a vocal patch. Devai says, 'I did background vocals, the high voice on the choruses. Kip and I were the main backing voices because he could hit high notes and so could I. He was my best friend on the tour'. Taylor says that 'We just thickened it up and it had the younger voices mixed in as well to give it more of the sound from the record'. On one occasion, Taylor was caught short with his patches and sound effects: 'I was up on this giant riser and back then, a sampler had discs that had to be loaded for the different sounds. We had played 'School's Out'. There was this one part where Alice was supposed to go across the stage, at which point I would play thunder noises. Little did I know, but something had gone wrong with the amps, so the crew were busy with that and they hadn't changed the disc. So Alice was lurking across the stage and I hit the key, and it goes 'School's Out'. He stops, looks up at me on the riser, and shrugs to say, 'What?' Later, he said, 'I was actually just trying to stop myself from laughing'. During the band introductions, Taylor would get a big cheer for his birthday every night. He says 'I had completely forgotten about that, but yes, that's right. I don't know where that started up'.

The guillotine was eagerly awaited every night, and Funaro, dressed as the priest, got a second brief moment in the limelight when he 'Got to walk Alice to the town square shaking a bible at him'. Ready to greet Alice would be Linda Albertano. She was in her element: 'I appeared in my bald-head wig as the black-robed executioner, I was Regina Dentata, the Queen of Teeth! Alice would be dragged to my guillotine and strapped down there while I raised the blade. Then, whoosh! As if by magic, his cranium rolled into the basket at my feet. I'd snatch it by the hair and make a dramatic show of kissing his dripping gory lips. I'd stride to the edge of the stage holding his head high, grinning diabolically. I would squeeze the head and the blood would spurt at the audience. I often feared Alice was taking his life into my hands each night on the guillotine'. As gory as this was, it seemed that the unexpected impaling of the cameraman in 'Go To Hell' was more shocking because many didn't know it was coming. The appearance of Mistress, the snake on 'Be My Lover' always got a great response too.

Then there was Kane Roberts, literally a show on his own but now memorably accessorised, courtesy of Rick Johnson from Los Angeles, who custom-made special guitars. Johnson explains what happened: 'In 1986, Alice Cooper's management contacted me to see if I could build custom guitars for Kane Roberts, so I met with them in Los Angeles to show them some of my guitars. We discussed what he wanted, and it was a machine gun guitar. I asked, 'Would you like it to shoot pyrotechnics such as flamethrowers, bottle rockets, roman candles?' 'Yes', they said. Tuning wasn't affected since all pyrotechnic devices were away from the tuners. A few weeks later, I delivered two guitars, one was a mock-up display guitar for promotional photos and the other one was a stage guitar, both with pyrotechnic effects. They also had installed rocket launchers that would launch Kane's autograph out into the crowd and float down with a parachute. I don't believe they used them, but they were installed. Two more Assault Guitars were made in the following months'.

Some of the press pointed out inherent issues in the show with regard to the treatment of women. The throwing around of the dummy in 'Cold Ethyl' and the strangling of the nurse in 'Dwight Fry' were obvious sticking points. Yet, by contrast, there was Alice singing his sympathies for abused women in 'Only Women Bleed'. Alice told *Rock Beat* (April 1987) that: 'One out of three concerts was picketed. Some shows they tried to stop at the city council; Mothers Against Lutherans Against Alice, stuff like that. Lots of people tried to stop the show, and in the weirdest places, like Las Vegas, Nevada. Did you know it's a very conservative place other than the Strip? In Daytona Beach, Florida, which is a party town. They were really out there in droves in St. Louis'.

Albertano recalls Alice surprising the pickets in one town: 'The Christian ladies were picketing and he invited some of them back into the green room and explained his philosophy and the cartoon side of things to them, and it all seemed very innocent. It was then I started to feel there was almost a Christian symbolism in the show. I mean, after he's executed, he does resurrect in a white suit for 'School's Out'. It's the Easter tale, in a way'.

Taylor affirms that 'There was always controversy. Trying to get through the border crossings with the snake was always an ordeal. We were in Toledo, Ohio and there was a giant protest in front so Sheryl went out there and calmed everybody down and said, 'Hey, you guys got this wrong; my husband's a church-going guy'. There was always that kind of stuff'.

The first American leg finished in November so the band jetted off to the UK. The first show was at Wembley Arena, London, on 23 November. It was a coolish start, says Mary: 'Everybody (in the audience) was doing this (arms folded). They were like, 'Well, let's see what you got!" Kane continues: 'I mean, Jeez, everybody was looking for the band from a while ago and they had gotten the sense there was a different sound and feel to everything. They wanted to see, what is this. On the surface, this may have seemed like some sort of weird experiment'. It was not what the band were used to at all. Mary adds: 'We were used to going onstage, the lights going out and the audience would roar. Wembley, it was silent so we looked at each other and said, 'Oh-oh, this is gonna be bad', you know? But as we got into it, got playing, the crowd went nuts. It was like, 'prove it to us', so once we proved it to them, it was OK'.

After the show, Kane got a shock: 'I put on my new black suede fringe jacket, we go downstairs and I open the door. There's bodyguards there and the parking lot is jammed with fans. The bodyguards had to escort me, but they were all ripping and grabbing at me. I lost most of the fringes on my jacket. I remember getting into the bus, saying, 'Wow, I'm like the Beatles". As the tour went on, he found that 'The thing about the British audiences Alice and I always noticed was they were the most informed. They were immersed in periodicals, not just videos'. Fans thronged at the hotels for autographs, with Albertano hugely popular. 'They loved the nurse and they would turn up at the hotel asking to have their thighs autographed and that sort of thing'. She noticed a certain conservatism in Ken Mary during the UK sojourn: 'He was the most conventional person on the tour. He was very upfront and when he went to England, he was shocked at people distributing Socialist Worker papers!'

After London, the tour moved to Edinburgh for two nights, where Devai got a new companion. 'The snake roomed with me for the next week. I had this boa constrictor in my bathroom and I had to keep the steam on and everything!' During the three nights at Birmingham Odeon, Devai ran into trouble after one of the shows: 'Larry Sapp, one of the techy guys (and a great guy), saved me from being beaten up by drunks in a bar. I was just too cute or something, so Larry saved me, along with Tom Haplin too'.

With little break, it was back to America for the second American tour, including Canada, with relatively few free days. The daily routines on show days were second nature and everything was taken in stride. Mary gives an example: 'Everything just went like clockwork. The crew was great – everything was very professional. There was one time in Rhode Island (Providence Civic Center on 19 February), I had food poisoning and I had a 103-degree fever, so I don't honestly remember the show. I was wrapped in a jacket, shivering and my drum tech pushed me up on the drum kit. I did the entire show, drum solo and everything. Everybody said I did great, but I don't even remember the show. That's how ingrained it was in our DNA at that point'.

Sylvia Dohi left after the Charleston show on 6 January. Karen Russell was ready to take her place for the next show, New Orleans, on 9 January. She recalls: 'When I auditioned, it was a girlfriend of mine in Los Angeles who told me about it; I didn't know who Alice Cooper was. My girlfriend played a prank on me. She said, 'You need to dress in black leather and you should get a whip because that's what they want'. I said OK, and there were hundreds of girls there to audition, it was crazy. I walked in. They were all sitting there, Alice, Shep Gordon and Toby Mamis. They asked me to get up and dance, but they said later on that as soon as I walked in the door, I stood out like a sore thumb. I was completely embarrassed because I was in like total S&M garb. I got the job, but I had no idea what it was. I was thinking more of musical theatre! I had to meet the band in New Orleans so I was standing there. The bus pulls up and all these guys came out with big hair and sunglasses on. I remember going, 'Oh my God, what did I just get myself into?'.

Russell took over the role of the whip dancer and 'Ethyl'. At Pittsburgh (16 February), there was a real issue for her during 'Cold Ethyl': 'The prop knife was a little sharp and it actually cut me just a little bit. Alice felt horrible. Of course, they were worried I was gonna sue them or something, but I didn't. But yeah, I did that whole hooker thing where he comes and kills me. So there were like three little parts'.

The band looked after Russell. She says, 'Paul Taylor and Kip were very sweet and protective over me. I remember when they were writing their album for Winger. We would be in the back and they were like, 'Hey, how about this song?' and I was like, 'Yeah, whatever, 'Seventeen', I guess it sounds OK!"

Albertano, too was impressed by Kip, in a different way: 'Gosh, he was as handsome as a movie star, one of the most beautiful men I have ever seen. he would come right up to you, put his toes against your toes (and of course, he had to look up to me), because he loved to invade your private space just to freak you out'.

The only one of the touring party to suffer an injury was Kip. He winces still at the memory: 'During 'Under My Wheels', I slipped on some fake blood and dislocated my knee, so I went down. Alice didn't realise I was hurt. He thought it was cool and put his foot on me as he was singing'. Paul Taylor was mystified: 'Everybody walked off the stage and I'm up on this 20-foot riser. I said, 'Why isn't he getting back up again?' Kip said, 'I couldn't get up because my knee was fucked. I finished the tour with a knee brace, sat in a chair kind of like a hospital thing. I had some workman's comp insurance and that financed the Winger demos'.

Times had changed on the dietary front since the 1970s. Albertano says, 'They were all into health. Kane would say to me, where did you score that low-fat cottage cheese? Everyone was trying to get their share of vegetables and protein'. Russell recalls: 'One time we were complaining we needed more vegetables on the rider. Alice was in the front seat of the bus and he turned round and said, 'This is so weird; we used to complain because there wasn't enough cocaine and alcohol'. Russell adds that: 'There was this idea that, you're on this rock tour with all these guys. Everyone thinks you're wild, right? But we were so clean and worked out. Kane Roberts and I used to work out a lot, so we were really close'.

Sadly there was one glitch in the relationships. Devai says, 'I was pretty much bullied on that tour. I'm an androgenous guy and (one of the tour party) was so threatened by me he was completely homophobic. There was the band, there were two girls and there was me. So they said, 'Trace, you have to dress with the band', because I wasn't going to dress with the girls, right? So I dressed with the band and (he) had a problem with that. I ended up having my own single dressing room, because he didn't want to dress with me. Can you believe that? He was such a dick to me the whole fucking tour'. Russell remembers it happening too: 'Trace wasn't treated really nicely. It always kind of bothered me. It wasn't down and out mean, but it was rude. It wasn't anything to do with Alice, though'.

The protests at venues continued throughout the tour, but what did the new recruit Karen Russell make of it all, being the onstage victim?' 'I'm in my twenties; I'm on tour; I'm having so much fun. It only dawned on me when I would look back at the photos and realise that people had looked at it as definitely alarming for women. At the time to me, it was a show, a role. My idea was that in 'Cold Ethyl', there was feeling there, and there was a little redemption. Alice was always very respectful. When we were together in close-up, he would always say, 'Are you OK?, are you alright?' He said I was the best one (in the role) other than his wife. He was one of my favourite bosses. He was a kind man'.

The last date should have been in Edmonton, Alberta, on 1 April, but the finale actually came a few months later. The Reading Festival appearance on 30 August was confirmed as the final *Nightmare Returns* show. There were unexpected difficulties for the production team as Devai remembers: 'I got a call from Larry Sapp (production team) – 'We are going to headline the Reading Festival, the Hells Angels want to do security for Alice and we can't stop them'. I will never forget those words. I mean, this was *our* security telling me that *we* can't stop them; what is that?!' The first shock for the band, though was when Devai turned up for the Reading rehearsal: 'I got married right after the first tour and for the rehearsal, I brought my wife. They couldn't believe I had got married because they thought I was gay. I shocked everybody'.

Albertano thought Reading was extraordinary: 'Oh my God, It seemed like thousands of people were there. The lights were so bright you couldn't see anything and you could just sort of feel the audience. It was this big thing that just seemed to spread out. There was this enormous energy'.

Perhaps not surprisingly, the only near foul-up came courtesy of the Hells Angels. Devai still winces at the memory: 'I had to do that photographer thing with the blood shooting out. So I am going on as a photographer for 'Go To Hell', and there's this giant ramp right up to the stage. I'm coming from my dressing room, but no one's walking with me as I go to do my thing. There's a gang of Hell's Angels in my way so I'm thinking, 'Oh my God', because my cue was coming up. This is the biggest show of the tour. I can't run by these guys because I can't be touched. So I'm stuck there in front of these guys and they're saying, 'No, no'. I tried to tell them who I was, but they can't hear me because it was so loud. Finally, Larry Sapp realises I am supposed to be there, so they run down and get them out of the way, and I'm running up the ramp and I just about made it. That was one of those crazy moments'.

Of the two 'metal' tours, *The Nightmare Returns* remains Mary's favourite: 'Back then I used to chew through learning stuff no problem at all. If I am 100% honest, the first tour to me was the most fun. I was really young, it was my first big tour so it was very special and it was a special band. Kip was a very special influence on me; he was older, so he used to give me advice on a lot of different things. It was maybe some of the most fun I've ever had in my entire life in terms of playing. I think Alice would tell you that the energy of that band was very powerful. Of course, I am not saying the band should have all the credit; Alice is a legend. But we did contribute something to give him the energy, the strength and the attitude for what that first tour was and the tone that was set. He was clean and healthy, but when he would get on that stage, he was like a madman; full of energy and life'. Alice gave all the band a big credit on 'Schools Out', but he always seemed to have an extra special regard for Mary, who says: 'I think he definitely appreciated the energy I brought to the show. If you think of the drummer, it's almost the engine of the car, the thing that holds it all together to some degree'.

Alice conservatively estimated to *Concert Shots* (November 1987) that 'The whole show was about $400,000 to put together. I'd say per week, it must have cost $100,000. It's the kind of thing where everybody's a specialist in the show, so everybody gets paid according to their speciality. It really works out well that way'.

It was all worth it because the tour was a huge success that did exactly what it set out to do by putting Alice back on top as a must-see performer. Kip recalls, 'We thought the tour was going to be like two months and it just blew up huge. It was really great to be with Alice Cooper as your mentor because it wasn't partying and getting drunk all the time. It was playing. There wasn't any self-sabotage; it was 'let's get this done'. He was like a big brother mentor, you know? There really is no one like him for sure'.

Taylor enjoyed the tour and also found a new writing partner: 'That first band was a great bunch, we got along super well, remaining friends to this day. We were out on that tour for pretty much a solid year. It was great, but also because Kip and I discovered we wrote really well together. We spent that year in motel rooms writing, just because we thought each other was talented, you know'.

Funaro says, 'I did gain a whole new respect and perspective for Alice from this experience. Hard workin', man! Great performance artist. Me? Gun for hire, will travel'.

Franz Harary loved working with Alice on the illusions and stunts. He amusingly adds that 'Alice Cooper is the kind of guy you want to call over to help you assemble your new barbecue grill. He's very down to earth, very easygoing. I had his number there for a while, and I could call him freely, and there was no pretentiousness'.

Could there ever be a reunion of this line-up? Ken Mary, for one, feels there could be more mileage even now in what they put together: 'I think if Alice went to tour Europe with that same band, we would do great at the major festivals. That approach would work in Europe, but I don't think it would do that well in the United States'.

Joe Louis Arena, Detroit, Michigan, 31 October 1986 (DVD)

The Nightmare Returns official video of the tour was recorded here and is an excellent record of the show, which never changed from one gig to the next. You get to appreciate just how well put together it all was when you see it in this level of detail. All the special effects and stunts can be seen in close-up, plus there's plenty of shots of the band and stage performers. The sound recording is excellent too.

Mary, while appreciating the scale of the gig, feels it came too early for the band: 'The nice thing about Detroit was that it was Alice's hometown and it was sold out at Joe Louis Arena. One time I think we played it three times in one year. For me personally, it was the biggest gig I had played to that point. If you look at the *The Nightmare Returns* DVD that was show number five, that was very, very early on. We ended up getting much, much better than that. In those first shows, that was a lot of pressure for Alice and I know he has talked about it, saying he was a little nervous and scared to go out there. This was the first tour he had ever done sober in his life. We were worried about what Alice was gonna be like. But I think that the energy that the band provided helped to make him a very aggressive Alice. He said, once he got into it, that it was the best he ever felt, very strong and powerful. But the first shows he was, I think, unsure about how he was going to handle it'.

Underlining Mary's points, Alice isn't as assured as he was later in the tour. On the encores, he sounds like he is running out of steam. This is understandable, with him having been away from the stage for so long and performing a strenuous set.

On the other hand, Funaro says, 'I have seen that Detroit show a hundred times. It was early in the tour and the band still felt some excitement for the whole thing'. Kip is positive too: 'Joe Louis Arena, live on MTV, with 20,000 people sold out. That was a fucking rush. It was really incredible, intense and awesome'. 'That was an incredible show', concurs Taylor, 'and of course, we were filming. It was just so cool to be playing those songs with such a legend'.

For one night, only Brian Nelson got to be the impaled cameraman, much to the chagrin of Devai: 'That was my gig, but that night they came to me and said Renfield is going to do it for the TV thing. I did it every other night'.

The audience reaction touched Linda Albertano: '20,000-strong three nights in a row. From behind the Sludge Monster's cage, I saw them all lift their lighters in salute to Alice'.

Cincinnati Gardens, Ohio, 6 March 1987

This show was heavily used for later B-sides, as follows: 'Schools Out' ('Freedom'), 'Ballad Of Dwight Fry' and 'Cold Ethyl' ('Poison'), 'Go To Hell' and 'Only Women Bleed' ('Bed Of Nails'), 'Billion Dollar Babies' and 'Under My Wheels' ('House Of Fire'). Some countries also had a single of 'Only My Heart Talkin'' which thoughtfully also used 'Only Women Bleed'.

Mary approves: 'I have heard the recording and we had definitely stepped it up by then. We really became a well-oiled machine as the tour went on'. The band are indeed on much better form than at Detroit. It's really noticeable just how tighter and more blistering the performances are, plus that Alice is also on better vocal form. He doesn't miss the top notes quite so much as he did at Detroit. The full show is easy to find online and the original Westwood One broadcast versions sound better than the remixes used as B-sides. This is a highly recommended show to pick up for your collection.

1987 and 1988 – Raise Your Fist and Yell and the In The Flesh Tour

Raise Your Fist and Yell (MCA)

Personnel:

Alice Cooper: vocals

Kane Roberts: guitar, backing vocals

Paul Taylor: keyboards

Kip Winger: bass, backing vocals, keyboards on 'Gail'

Ken Mary: drums

With:

Robert Englund: voice on 'Lock Me Up'

Produced in June/ July 1987 by Michael Wagener at Amigo Studios, Hollywood

Release date: 5 September 1987

Highest chart places: UK: 48, USA: 73

Running time: 36:53

Kane feels that the album was a step up from *Constrictor:* 'It was critical that we heavied up for *Raise Your Fist And Yell*. You can hear that Alice and I were in full stride. That's a very consistent record'.

Having the *The Nightmare Returns* tour band on the record (well, most of them) was a major plus. Kane agrees that 'It was a better album for having a band playing on it. We had just finished the tour, and we hit the ground running into the studio. The musicianship on it is stunning, but you've got to dig a little bit to get it in the mix. We played through that album like a perfectly oiled machine and Alice's vocals are incredible'. 'We were very excited', enthuses Kip. 'We were like, OK, let's go in and kill. I thought there was really cool stuff on there, like 'Freedom''.

Paul Taylor was keen to write for the album: 'Alice came to the band and said we were going to be doing a new record. I wrote five song ideas that were really cool, and Alice wanted to write a song called 'Technophobia'. So, I wrote this idea with my buddy Danny Lux. I gave our ideas to Alice and he really liked two of them. But in the end, I never got any of my song ideas on there'. Taylor's musical contributions were all overdubs: 'I went in for a couple of days to do my parts. I added some beds, pads and strings in the background here and there for some vibe. Just rich-sounding mellow sounds that blend in, as opposed to piano or percussive sounds or parts. It was Michael Wagener and me working together. He had production ideas, but nobody sat there saying to me do this or do that. It was very quick, easy and fun. That was the first record I ever played on. I don't think much of my work on it, but there are some cool songs'.

One who didn't make it into the studio was Arti Funaro, which still rankles with him: 'I wasn't on the album for only one reason. Alice told me that he'd call me when it was time for guitars. Someone else made sure that never happened. Very insecure, enough said. I never listened to the whole album; I didn't even own a copy'. Ken Mary diplomatically says, 'I think it was just a question of the need. Kane was gonna play those solos and he had his rhythms. I think, honestly, it was just a question of something that wasn't going to be easy to work in – budgets influencing how much money and time you have to spend. It was just easier for Kane to play the rhythm and the solos'. One who did feel Funaro deserved to be on the record was Kip: '*Raise Your Fist* would have been improved with Arti's guitar playing added to it. The unsung heroes are the guys holding the fort in the background and Arti came from that era. He played an SG and he had a very authentic tone. He could have brought the authenticity of the '70s onto that album'.

Kip continues, saying that it was Alice and Kane making the calls on the album: '[They] had a quarantine on the songwriting. I would have loved to get in there, I had some good riffs, but Kane was pretty protective of that. It was the same with him wanting to play all the guitars. He was like, 'this is my baby'.'

Most of the album was written during the *The Nightmare Returns* tour. Twenty songs were taken into the studio and the best ten were selected for recording. Having 'salvaged' *Constrictor,* Michael Wagener was back again as producer. Mary was new to his methods but was impressed: 'He was a total professional. We were all pretty young and I just remember that we were joking the whole time in the studio. Michael has a great sense of humour, so, at the end of the day, we would comment, 'Wow, we got four songs done'. You didn't realise you had done so much work because it had been so much fun'.

The first job was to get Mary's drums down: 'The drum tracks were finished in four days. I would do three or four songs a day, which was pretty quick for that time period. As far as the rest of the album, I think it was about a month and a half, a fairly rapid production'.

First impressions were not good; it was a crass album title for a start. Either of the two working titles, *Summer Blood* or *Sex, Death And Money* (later used as a song title), would have been better. Then there was the awful cover with the raised fist and Alice's cartoon face. Fortunately, the album delivered much more than the cover or even *Constrictor* promised. Side one's songs are like an upgraded *Constrictor*, very good without being great. But on side two, some of the Cooper magic of old appears. What is, for the most part, a connected song suite has guile, spirit and conviction that surprises and delights. The comeback, at last, seemed it might have longevity, with echoes of the past in convincing new material. Mary feels that: 'It's an interesting record with a lot of variation on it. There are things that are a little more commercial and there are things that are definitely not meant to be commercial, like 'Gail' and 'Roses On White Lace'. The best thing about that record for me personally was that Kane, Alice and Michael Wagener were, within reason, letting me do what I wanted to do. They wanted all the musicians to shine on the record'.

Alice for one felt pleased with the results: 'In contrast, *Constrictor* sounds, in my opinion, flaccid', he told *Crash* (1987). 'The new one is exactly what I want to do right now. It's hard rock to a degree that I can't go beyond. The PMRC will hate it. There's a song on there about them called 'Freedom'. There's a ballad on there, but it's totally deranged. The whole side two is like a heavy psychodrama'.

The drum sound was also something Alice picked up on. He told *Metal Hammer* (September 1987) that: 'I'm one hundred per cent happy with the drum sound on this one. Simmons-type drums dominate the *Constrictor* album. That was Beau Hill's idea and he started the production on the album until Michael Wagener took over. This time around, we've used real nasty rock'n'roll type drums, a definitive kind of sound that suits our kind of music the best'. Talking about his drumming, Mary rightly says that: 'I think I pushed the bar forward in metal drumming for sure at that time. One of the main things I was known for was double bass drums interacting with the toms in a very musical way'.

As good a producer for metal/rock as Wagener is, Kip feels the final product could have been better: 'I have always wanted to remix that album because, when it came out, the bass was gone. The mix didn't do that album justice. It doesn't have enough balls; it could have been much more organically heavy. I don't know if anyone else will tell you that, but we were all disappointed'. However, Kip adds a happy memory of the sessions: 'Alice and I singing backups on *Constrictor* and *Raise Your*

Fist, singing so high. I mean, like just screaming. I got such a headache from doing them. To be able to say I stood next to Alice and sung all that shit is just amazing'.

'Freedom' (Cooper/ Roberts)

'I wrote it on the level of saying, look, anybody that starts out with a premise that all kids are created stupid, I can't understand it, but that's really what they say! They don't understand that these kids grew up with the *Friday the 13th* movies. They understand satire; they understand humour. They understand what Alice is about'. (Alice to *The Georgia Straight*, December 1987)

Alice came up with this song response to the Parents Music Resource Center (PMRC) who had formed in 1985 with the goal of increasing parental control over music. The furore was kick-started with the so-called 'filthy fifteen' songs identified by the PMRC. None of Alice's songs were in the fifteen and little attention seems to have been given by them to his records. His concerts, now that was different!

This 'anthem' gets off to a great start. The intro with Mary's drums is more potent than anything on *Constrictor.* Once Kane and Kip come in, it's a beast of a sound; those three really did have something special together. Alice sounds better already, too, with a sparkling delivery in most of his range with just a little roughness at the top.

The Liberty Bell ringing (from 2:20) is a little indistinct and could have done with being mixed up to give it more clarity. Overall this is a muscular piece that has power and conviction. It's not a classic, but good enough for the genre and the tone they were going for.

It references the title of the album in the lyrics and this perhaps would have been a better title for the track itself with some lyrical adjustments. An edited version was released as a single with a promo video made to support it.

'Lock Me Up' (Cooper/ Roberts)

Ken Mary loves it: 'That's one of my favourite ones. It has a drum intro that I still like to this day. I go back and listen, and, you know, for being young, that was pretty advanced stuff. We had the song to listen to, so Kane said, 'Hey, I'd like you to do a drum intro'. We had already rehearsed the song, and we put the drum intro at the top'.

Mary's stunning intro shows why he was such an asset. The surging riff from Kane that follows it is pretty good, too, with some squealing lead lines for dressing. It all goes a bit awry with the comic cut to Robert Englund's cameo, though Alice has the wit to give the one-word reply of 'Guilty'.

The verses have a rolling rhythm with a similar pacing to Alice. The chorus is another gang-style 'Raise your fist' pumper and frankly, it doesn't hit the mark. Kane gets off a good solo and the Mary/ Winger rhythm section is superbly tight. Other than that, it's an average tune at best.

'Give The Radio Back' (Cooper/ Roberts)

'There's so little rock on the radio now; it's all *Graceland* and Whitney Houston. Nothing's really for the kids. I wrote the song because that's the way it was when I was young', recalled Alice (*Everyday*, January 1988). Sadly his song doesn't sit in the same exalted company as his previous radio hits. Some radio tuning opens it, and you wonder if there was a thought (Kiss, 'Detroit Rock City' style) to include an Alice hit here. But no, it's over in a flash and into the song proper.

It's an interesting composition as it eschews the obvious gang-style choruses and opts for a more restrained tone. This is odd, given the demonstrative message. The mid-paced tempo and grinding rhythm guitars work reasonably enough, with Kane overdubbing squealing lead fills for contrast and colour. He sparkles over the outro, which otherwise is a fairly bland fade-out.

'Step On You' (Cooper/ Roberts)

'It was written on the first day we got together to write songs', says Kane. 'It wasn't used on *Constrictor*', says Alice, 'because it sounded too much like 'Give It Up'. We didn't want to piss the fans off by giving them two tracks that sounded so similar on one album'. (*Metal Hammer*, September 1987)

So if it wasn't deemed as good as 'Give It Up', was it worth resurrecting for *Raise Your Fist*? If we are comparing the two, then this one is the better song. The metre of the song with Alice's vocals is interesting, with a deliberate enunciation that matches the riff. The chorus is pretty much an extension of the verses and the first variation of any note comes in the second verse (0:47) when Kane adds a harmony guitar part that works well.

The song shifts gears at 1:34 for some plunging riffs and harder-edged vocals. The surprise element comes after a section that sounds like the guitar is coiling up, ready to snap. Then, at 2:33, there is a rush as Mary is unleashed. From here, it almost sounds like they have segued into a different song. This end section is a thunderous roar, with Kane on fire.

'Not That Kind Of Love' (Cooper/ Roberts)

The opening comic book line doesn't promise much. Fortunately, the song recovers somewhat. The stop-start rhythms are a different touch and the vocal melodies are good. The chorus sees Alice ably backed by Kane and Kip's backing vocals which give things a lift. It's all still rooted in the heavy metal idiom, but they don't forego the melodic touches.

Kane's solo is a bit metal by numbers and it does underline one of the issues about the 'metal Alice' albums. We are used to more diversity in the lead guitar parts but too often, Kane has to fall back on the metal tropes that, in fairness, these sorts of songs require. It's an average end to side one, but it's listenable enough.

'Prince Of Darkness' (Cooper/ Roberts)

The song is (just about) featured in the film *Prince Of Darkness,* and was the last track recorded for the album. It's also the one Alice picked as his favourite and he is right as it's the best on the album, along with pretty much all of side two, which is superior to side one. Mary agrees that: 'The second side is a little bit more artistic. We were less worried about having to do something that had commercial value. To me, that's the best art, when you are not doing something from a commercial standpoint'.

Kane reasons: 'You can tell Alice and I were in story mode. We were thinking like, let's create this world, talking about Satan, but it gets darker as we talk about a bride getting married and murdered. We were doing grand guignol. It feels like a deeper project on side two'. Mary also picks up on the change in atmosphere: 'It's definitely a different mood on that track. It's a dark song, one of the moodiest tracks on the record'.

It gets off to a great start, Mary's cavernous drums rolling into the most intense riff yet, which is set off by a well-judged melodic lead fill from Kane. As soon as Alice comes in, 'An angel fell one stormy night', you can hear clearly that he is responding more to this song than anything on side one (save perhaps 'Freedom'). The verse lyrics and delivery are the best yet, while the build-up to the chorus from Alice and the band is masterful. The rising power and tension are well done, with Alice imperious as Kane picks out a mournful guitar line and then the perfect release in the perversely euphoric chorus.

The bridge (2:12) doesn't let us down. It's a considered instrumental break with sustained notes from Kane over Mary's steady toms. Kane builds the notes up to an excellent solo where he seems to throw every trick in his arsenal at it! He finishes it off with a return to the song's melody. This is his best work yet on the album!

Being the longest song on the album helps things breathe and stretch out, which is fine because there is more going on here than can easily be done in three or four minutes. The last part of the song has a different atmosphere to it at first – 'He fears the light, he fears the truth' – and again, you sense Alice is enjoying trying out some different tones. This part is effectively an interlude before the last assault, while it's good to hear Taylor's keyboards here adding some welcome textures.

After several choruses, we get a slice of vintage Alice for the outro. Taylor's string synths are the main backing sound, with Kane strumming over the top. It's a chilled-out cinematic ending as Alice almost speaks the closing lines, with that sibilance on 'prince' at its most audible.

'Time To Kill' (Cooper/ Winger/ Roberts)
A naggingly familiar riff opens the song' before a grinding riff underpins the scene-setting first verse. It's a short verse, so they hit the first chorus fast, and it's a really good one. A very catchy melody over slabs of metal guitar. Kane's solo is a bit metal-by-numbers but otherwise serviceable.

The catchy melodic side of the song never overpowers the more basic rhythmic side making for a well-balanced track. But it's that strong chorus that keeps your attention. Kip's credit speaks volumes as a clue to where the increased melodic sensibilities have come from.

'Chop, Chop, Chop' (Cooper/ Roberts)
Kane: 'I love that song. Alice's assistant (Renfield) was a huge 'classic Alice' fan and he would be very critical of songs as we wrote them. That was his favourite on the record. He said, 'To me, that's Alice'. Mary isn't so sure about the song, though: 'That's not a favourite, but it definitely has a memorable hook. That's probably why it's not my favourite because it's just so easy to lock in. I feel like the other ones are a little more thought-provoking, I guess'.

In the lyrics, Alice adopts the persona of The Creeper, aka The Ripper, a 'homicidal genius' and 'engine of destruction'. Rather than go for a sinister, creepy musical backdrop, they came up with a powerful earworm with a very catchy hook. The combination of the music and Alice's strident confessional lyrics makes for an irresistible track.

Kane's doubled opening riff is terrific, punctuated by Mary's drum fills. As soon as Alice comes in, you can tell he is relishing the song and his performance This is one of the problems he has in his metal years. He doesn't get to adopt personas and perform in the way that he has been used to. But he is seriously on form and the chorus doubles down on that; it's an exultant pride in his activities that makes you recoil but want to hear more about the 'symbiotic function', which is the connection between killer and victim.

Alice hits his highest note on the album on this one – 'I take her for a little ride', his voice flying off into the night. Uniquely there is no guitar solo, which keeps the pace and momentum going without diversion. What we do get is a brooding instrumental break (from 1:33) which is the bridge to part two of the song. This is a welcome surprise, a different feel, as The Creeper/Ripper approaches his next victim. The chilling horror as he surveys her 'standing on the corner' is brought home when he misreads the name on her anklet – 'It spelled M-A-R-Y, Gail'.

'I thought it was hilarious, you know when he spells MARY – Gail', says Ken Mary. 'I thought it was funny that my name ended up on the record!' It is, though, a classic piece of Alice's writing to show the psychotic side of the killer in this reveal. The growing frenzy in his voice on the fadeout leaves you to imagine and shudder at what might be happening.

'Gail' (Cooper/ Roberts/ Winger)

The most distinctively different cut on the album. Alice told *Metal Hammer* (September 1987) that, 'The lyrics are really sick, and as a contrast, we wanted the music to come across nice 'n' sweet. Kip had a real sickly sweet melody kicking around that was just right'.

Kip recalls he came up with it by request: 'They said, 'Hey man can you write something classical weird?' I said, 'Yeah, I can do that'. So I was lucky to get a little piece on there. It's almost classic Cooper. It would have fitted in on something like *Nightmare* particularly'. Mary concurs: 'It's definitely old school Cooper. It's a cool piece. Kip was always doing compositions on the tour bus'.

Kip plays the keyboards himself, which pleased Taylor, who might have expected to do it: 'Thank god Kip played the keyboards on it because it was tricky to play in true Kip fashion. He writes some of the coolest stuff'.

The eerie wind sound that helps the segue from 'Chop, Chop, Chop' conjures up images of what has happened. The treat here is Kip's cinematic composition which gives it a real *Phantom Of The Opera* feel. It's just Alice and Kip for the first part of the song, which is a ballad of sorts; exactly the kind of 'ballad' Alice could do with in his set to this day. He has a forlorn, regretful quality in his voice and you wonder if this is a different personality of The Creeper that we are hearing. Having hit us hard with that anklet reading in 'Chop, Chop, Chop', Alice manages to top that with the unforgettable, 'A dog dug up a bone and wagged his tail'.

The second half is a full-on outro, with Kane's layered guitars eventually making way for a brief return to Kip/Alice's deadly slow waltz. While it is a highlight of the album, Kip is not happy with how Wagener mixed and produced it: 'I didn't like the way he handled the keyboards. It's a very particular way that that should have sounded. It's like Bela Lugosi sitting in the harpsichord. That's what the piece is. I delivered it the way I wanted it. Michael took my midi file and stacked up a bunch of samples and stuff without dynamics, so it doesn't do what it's supposed to musically. My version was alive; it was organic'. It's still a highlight of the album, at any rate.

'Roses On White Lace' (Cooper/ Winger/ Roberts)

'This guy's a romantic, you know? He's so crazy, he looks at this blood and all he sees are roses. (It's) this whole thing about him not knowing that it's really blood. For him, he's painted these lovely roses on this white dress. So he's really a psycho'. (Alice to *Kerrang*, October 1987)

Kip managed to get on the credits with Alice and Kane for this one: 'He would bring me in every now and then because he trusted me – 'So what do you think of this? What do you think of that? Maybe we should go here?"

The heavy riffing returns, along with Mary's outstanding drums to the fore again. He is absolutely blistering on this, somehow topping anything he has played elsewhere on the album. He remains proud of his work: 'That was something where even Michael Wagener said, 'this is Ken's song'. I have drummers that, to this day, ask, 'What happened? Did you eat extra Wheaties that morning?' It was great for its time; it was cutting-edge and moved the bar forward'.

The song itself is good enough but lacks the range of colour and diversity that has spoiled us on much of side two. Alice's vocals sound a little repetitive, and the chorus doesn't stand out. It's the musical skill that works on this one. Kane's solo is good, working well over the rhythm track; he blends the two parts together well. There's a nice touch with the deeper voice doubling Alice on parts of the lyrics, which gives a sense of the demonic at work.

Once we get to the outro, it sounds like they have run out of steam or ideas on how to finish the track. It just kind of fades out and sadly, it's unsatisfying.

Alleged outtake
'Bad Girl In Love'

No further information is known on this one and Ken Mary is completely unaware of it: 'I don't believe there were any extra tracks recorded'. That could mean there was a demo by Kane and Alice, but Kane is unaware of the song too.

1988 recordings
'Under My Wheels' (Michael Bruce/ Dennis Dunaway/ Bob Ezrin)
The opening classic from *Killer* was re-recorded for *Decline And Fall Of Western Civilisation Part II*. Along for the session with Alice and Kane were Steve Steele (bass) and Victor Russo (drums). The presence of these two, points to it being recorded during sessions for Kane's debut solo album, *Kane Roberts*.

Joining Alice and his alumni on the track are Axl, Slash and Izzy from Guns 'N' Roses. While Alice and Axl trade vocals effectively enough, there's a sense of there being too many guitarists.

Kane says it didn't take long to put down: 'We all knew each other. Slash is one of the nicest guys I ever met, and also I got along with Axl. We all met at the studio and we all knew the song. We rehearsed it once or twice, then recorded it. I loved trading licks with Slash'.

It was produced in early 1988 by Jim Faraci at White Crow Audio, Burlington and Rumbo Recorders, Canoga Park, so there must have been overdubs. It's good, but the original is stunning.

'I Got A Line On You' (Randy California)
This song, originally by Spirit, was featured in the film *Iron Eagle II*. It was released in November 1988, straddling the *Raise Your Fist* and *Trash* eras. You can see where Alice has come from and where he is heading, albeit with a cover of a favourite song. It must be a favourite because he returned to it again with The Hollywood Vampires.

It was produced in mid-1988 by Richie Zito at One On One Studios in Los Angeles. Alice was backed with a top-notch group of musicians, which hinted at the *Trash* model: Adrian Vandenburg (guitar), Rudy Sarzo (bass), Mike Baird (drums) and old friends Flo & Eddie on backing vocals. Sarzo says that: 'We were all in the studio, the old-school way. Cooper's record company called me up to do the session'. Sarzo adds it was a one-off, with no thought of the project leading to anything long-term.

It's a professional version of the song, punchy and hard-hitting, but it lacks the finesse or colour of the original. This, to some extent, was addressed on the Vampires' version, but the best is still the Spirit original. There was a video of the song which got heavy rotation.

In The Flesh Tour
15 October 1987 (Ventura, California) to 6 May 1988 (Brussels, Belgium)

Setlist: 'Teenage Frankenstein', 'No More Mr Nice Guy', 'Billion Dollar Babies', 'Is It My Body', 'I'm Eighteen', 'Go To Hell', 'Prince Of Darkness', 'Chop, Chop, Chop', 'Gail', 'Roses On White Lace', 'Only Women Bleed', 'Devil's Food', 'The Black Widow', 'Dead Babies', 'Killer', 'School's Out', 'Freedom', 'Under My Wheels'
Occasionally played: 'He's Back (The Man Behind The Mask)'
Musicians: Kane Roberts (lead guitar), Arti Funaro aka Johnny Dime (guitar), Paul Taylor aka Horowitz (keyboards), Steve Steele (bass), Ken Mary (drums)
Stage Performers: Linda Albertano, Trace Devai (backing vocals as well), Karen Russell, Lisa Oakley (replaced Karen Russell for European dates)

Alice outlined his intentions to *Kerrang* (October 1987): 'We're going to be incorporating more of *Constrictor*, more of the new album, and start dropping off the older stuff'. Kip Winger feels the 'go with the new' was partly down to Kane: 'He was like, 'Come on, let's do our songs'. He had a big influence on that". Swapping out some of the old classics for others was a good move. 'Public Animal #9' was close to making the final cut. Also very close to making the set, it seems, was 'Unfinished Sweet'. Karen Russell says that: '*Raise Your Fist And Yell* wasn't the big hoopla (that the previous tour was). I remember being at this rehearsal and thinking, oh my God, this is what happens when you have more money to spend on a show. They were going to bring in this thing of toothpaste and a prop. There was this big rehearsal for like a week, then they nixed it and it never made it in'. The big visual effect change was the guillotine being replaced by the gallows. Devai found the 'new' execution underwhelming. 'It wasn't as dramatic as the guillotine',he says.

The key musical changes were the *Killer* and *Nightmare* song inclusions to give the live set more focus. The set did, though, feature more new material (including 'Teenage Frankenstein') than *The Nightmare Returns* tour, with 'Prince Of Darkness' getting an extended outro, a minute longer, to cover the onstage visuals. Although the old classics were reduced somewhat, Arti Funaro's perception was that the old tunes were in the ascendant. 'Slowly, they started bringing back more old tunes and I did not like that direction. I found myself loving Heavy Metal'.

Ken Mary feels the balance was right with six new songs now in the set: 'There was a little more confidence in the (new) material because it was more of a band, so to speak, at that point. We had worked the songs out live as a band. It added a certain energy to what was going on and also where Alice was headed at that moment. It was very descriptive; he was getting further into horror movies'.

The original intention was for a European tour starting in September, but all of the dates were cancelled. Russell says that instead, the rehearsals ended up being in September/October in Los Angeles.

Fans did get extra recordings of interest to tide them over while they waited. Kane's debut, *Kane Roberts*, came out on MCA on 21 September. Alice co-wrote the song 'Full Pull' and Kip Winger popped by to add backing vocals. On bass was Steve Steele, while on drums was Victor Ruzzo. Steele got the gig on the *In The Flesh* tour, while Ruzzo popped up later, along with Steele, on the re-recording of 'Under My Wheels' with Guns 'N' Roses.

Alice was enthused to be getting back out on the road with a mostly familiar band. Pseudonyms were again adopted by Funaro and Taylor. Mary feels that: 'Arti relished in being his character. On this tour, he was Johnny Dime; he had these characters he liked to make up. I think he definitely enjoyed the whole theatrical aspect of it'. Funaro, typically, has his own unique perspective: 'Johnny Dime was a protective device. Protection from embarrassment. If there had been a third tour, I would have changed my name again. Alice thought that was just silly. I had my reasons that were not'.

Taylor was, this time round, called by his real name Paul Horowitz. He had decided to get together with Kip in their own band called Winger.

While Taylor was able to do the tour, Kip was not. Taylor says that 'We had talked to Alice, and of course, we were concerned. We told him we had written some songs and Atlantic had signed us. He was 100% supportive'. For Kip, it had been a tough decision: 'I thought to myself, once a side-man, always a side-man. My whole mission in life was to do my own music and front my own band. There was no disrespect intended; the most supportive of the decision was Alice. He was like, 'Absolutely, you should go do your own band; good luck'. So while me and Reb were writing, Paul went out on tour and then left".

'Kip made his decision to leave after we had made the record', says Mary. 'He told me, 'Hey, I'm not gonna be doing the tour'. I was extremely disappointed because he is a really good friend and we had so much fun on the first tour, I was really going to miss him a lot'. Replacing Kip was Steve Steele from Kane's band Criminal Justice. Mary recalls that 'There wasn't an audition because Kane felt comfortable with Steve, so he pulled him into the tour. Steve did a great job, so we became really great friends. We would go sightseeing together, out for dinners and all that stuff'. Funaro was OK with the swap, too: 'Steve joined the ranks of the backing band and all was well. He is one of the nicest people I have ever met'. Taylor adds that: 'Kane and Steve used to work out together, doing all the muscle man stuff'.

Also returning (initially) were Trace Devai, Linda Albertano and Karen Russell. As well as the Frankenstein monster, Devai had two other big, though somewhat static, roles: 'As Prince of Darkness, I don't think I really did anything; I just stood there. I also did The Black Widow and I just stood there. It was so weird being in that outfit. I did backing vocals again too'. Russell was sent shopping for new stage clothes: 'The prostitute costume made sense. Alice said for me to go to Trashy Lingerie *to* pick out something and I said, 'People actually wear this stuff?'.' Albertano was the executioner again: 'I have a memory of wearing the claw eyepatch and the black leather hood. My part in the said hanging was far less dramatic'.

Alice was more enthused than ever by the band, as he explained to *Faces* (1988): 'This band is great. We have a musical rehearsal for three weeks before we go into dress rehearsals, and this band has got all the stuff down in two days. I can say, 'OK, take it from the third bar of the second part of the song', and they start right there. Everybody knows the stuff backwards; I went into this thing on a good level. I took songs like 'Eighteen', 'Billion Dollar Babies' – songs that you have to do onstage, and left them alone with the songs for a week. I said: 'Kane, just rearrange them. Play 'em the way you'd play 'em in 1988'. I'd come back in and the song was right there. It was totally the same song, only now it's got the slant, the '88 kind of sound that I want to hear. I said: 'I don't wanna do them like the record at all. Please don't feel confined by the arrangements. It's like clay, just play with it until you like it'. Then I came back in and polished it up, said, 'OK, let's lose that, let's take that back in', so you got a brand new sound. A song like 'Public Animal #9' or 'Under My Wheels' suddenly sounds like it was written last week'.

Initial press reaction was positive, with the usual focus on visuals and effects. In November 1987 *Scene* reported that: 'Alice will be pulling out all the stops for his live appearance at Public Hall this Saturday night (14 November). He has resurrected the gallows and the 13-foot black widow spider from the *Nightmare* tour. The previous night's dress rehearsal was 'like Christmas morning' for him because he got to see all of the special effects at work for the very first time'.

By the time a few dates had taken place, the blood and gore aspects of the show were drawing criticism. *Detroit Free Press* (October 1987) focussed on the key problem area: 'While performing a suite of songs about a psychotic killer from his new album, *Raise Your Fist and Yell*, Cooper pretends to stalk, attack and murder a female character. He winds up singing his 1975 hit, 'Only Women Bleed', as she lies on the stage floor at his feet. This is an admittedly calculated shock designed to create outrage and publicity, just as Cooper did with his '70s productions. But there's a certain amount of tastelessness here; chopping up an inanimate object is one thing, but staging an assault is another. Slash movies may be more realistic, but they're not real-life'. The *Montreal Gazette* (February 1988) felt that: 'The newer songs lack the gallows humour of earlier material like 'Cold Ethyl' or 'School's Out'. The stage scene of a prostitute having her throat slashed and lying dead for ten minutes while the band played on was not only unfunny and uncathartic, but a dumb, stupid lesson in misogyny for impressionable headbangers'.

Alice himself was aware that they may have gone too far. He told *The Province* (December 1987): 'That one section (a trilogy featuring 'Chop Chop Chop') of the show leaves a bad taste in everyone's mouth because it really is too splatter-oriented. It's a little too graphic and that's been one of the criticisms of the show'. Another issue *The Province* added to the mix was the styling of the music, where they felt that the new material was inferior and that the band's, '747-roar drained the pop blood out of tunes such as 'I'm Eighteen' and 'Is It My Body'".

The 'weeding out' of older material hadn't happened. Funaro was frustrated: 'We couldn't change anything. Same exact show every night. We added 'Freedom', but it didn't last very long. I can only speak for myself here, but the second tour was like a London stage show that lasted a bit too long in its run. We knew every note we had to play, but the life of the show suffered a tiny bit'. Indeed Funaro has trouble thinking of anything positive about the tour: 'I would say that with the exception of many of Ken's drum solos (which were top-notch), there were no musical bright spots that I remember. I really wished that we would have played more songs from the two new albums. 50/50 would have been nice. What I do remember is calling out a number after the last encore nightly, which was the number of shows we had left before I could just go home'.

Alice, meanwhile, was relishing the new lease of life. He detailed his routine for *Concert Shots* (November 1987): 'I don't use a dressing room; I use the bus, always. I think once you get into the dressing room, you kinda lose your energy. You get too distracted by all the people around, you know? But anyway, I usually go to the video store, get my videos, I come back to the hotel, usually do about two or three interviews, and then close my eyes for about 20 minutes at 5:00. I wake up just in time to watch *Wheel of Fortune*, or, if I'm really lucky, *Divorce Court* or *People's Court* — those are the ones that get me up for the show. Then I get down to the bus and I have one candy bar, Hershey's dark chocolate, I watch my martial arts movie, put my makeup on, and then I'm ready. For about an hour, I sit there and turn into Alice'.

Several shows were cancelled in November due to sluggish ticket sales, and main support act Ace Frehley dropped out. Guns 'N' Roses came in for some December dates but didn't impress Russell at first: 'I would be backstage warming up for my whip dance and the guys from Guns 'N' Roses would be like all screwed up on stuff. I had no idea; I was literally like, 'Why do they stink?' I just thought they didn't take a bath. I thought they were a bunch of losers because they were just a mess. Then later, I was backstage when they did 'Sweet Child O' Mine' and that changed me. I told Kip, 'I think this band's gonna hit big', then six months later, they were the biggest thing ever'.

The unexpected death of Alice's father, Ether Furnier, on 13 December saw understandable postponements. Russell says, 'We took a few days off so he could go to the funeral'. Devai recalls that 'We were stuck in a little town (Muskegon, Michigan) and we all hung out'. Alice returned to the stage on 17 December for the gig in St. Paul, Minnesota.

Funaro, by now, felt, 'The old songs just ended up sounding like old songs. They didn't have the power of the new stuff. I wasn't really a fan of Alice's before I met him. The older stuff, newer stuff, really didn't matter. I was a bit disappointed when the higher-ups started bringing back the old songs. Maybe ticket sales were slipping or something. I really wasn't told why. I also didn't really care. A gig's a gig. You do it well, and professionally at all times. I was digging the Marshalls and the power. Simply, it was a pro gig, that I took. I'll play whatever you tell me to play if your check doesn't bounce'.

The tour began to run out of steam and Albertano and Devai were let go at Christmas 1987. Albertano says: 'An Alaskan performance (Anchorage, 1 January) was added as a surprise extension around Christmas 1987. It may have been left off of the official itinerary as it came up suddenly and unexpectedly. I remember Kane Roberts teasing me about the deaths of Buddy Holly, Ritchie Valens and the Big Bopper in their last unfortunate airplane ride. The thought of flying into a snowstorm in Alaska in the midst of darkest winter utterly unnerved me. As I'd already made plans to spend Christmas with my family, I elected to go home. A burly stagehand took over the role of The Executioner'.

Devai was also replaced: 'One of the crew ended up taking my place. My last date was at Christmas time. They said the tour wasn't really doing well. I learned a lot from touring with Alice Cooper. He's a creative person and sees it all. I always felt he took care of me and always made sure everything was good with me'.

Russell, whose key high-profile presence was harder to replace, was retained. Without Devai (and, of course, Kip), who then was left to hit the high notes? Taylor doesn't remember but offers that 'Kane sang and I was singing, although I couldn't hit the high stuff'.

The tour rattled on into 1988, with Motorhead as special guests. One stand-out night was 26 February when Izzy, Slash and Axl from Guns 'N' Rose came on for the encore at Long Beach Arena. They joined in on a riotous 'Under My Wheels'. *Kerrang* (April 1988) got the details from Alice: 'It was a bit nerve-racking last night because it's the first time I've done a duet with anyone on stage. But it was time for the stage to be shared. See, Alice never shares the stage with anyone, but it went pretty good last night and it was time to do something new'.

Alice left MCA at the end of February, leaving him playing the remaining dates promoting an album on his former label. Fortunately, all those dates were in Europe, where he was assured of sell-out shows. By now, things were starting to fly with Winger and Taylor experienced his first clash of commitments: 'Kip had scheduled a photo shoot, but I was supposed to fly to Europe with Alice. The shoot was in New York but I was in LA, so I tried to schedule it, so I did the photo shoot and then got a plane to join Alice, but they couldn't do it. I ended up flying to New York for the shoot, then back to LA and then from there to London'.

The European tour this time included other countries as well as the UK. The London Wembley Arena show saw the reported incident when the safety harness for the hanging failed, leaving Alice allegedly bruised and shaken. At least three of the band don't remember it at all. Funaro says: 'That never happened. When Alice did the hangings, he was attached via a back brace, never by the neck. It just looks like a hanging'. Taylor says, 'There were some close calls. All those tricks used to freak me out watching even though I knew they were fairly safe'. Mary is unaware of the incident but observes: 'You know, if something like that happened, I could not have known about it. The way that we operated as a band was like if you weren't dead; you were playing the next show. I don't care what happened if it was food poisoning or you had a broken arm and you were the drummer – you were going to play. So Alice could nearly have been killed, but nobody would have batted an eyelid'.

The UK dates were dogged by adverse press reactions to the gore. Sensationalist press had served Alice well in the past, but this time it felt like there was some justification for the criticism. Prominent among the critics was Sheffield's Labour MP David Blunkett. *The Daily Mirror* (6 April 1988) set the scene with their comments that the first UK gig had seen young fans faint, throw up and get 'splattered with buckets of blood'. Blunkett called for a ban on the act, saying: 'I'm horrified by his behaviour; it goes beyond the bounds of entertainment. It's an indication of the sick society we're moving into, and something drastic should be done to protect young people from paying for this sort of obscenity'. *The Daily Mirror* helpfully added further details: 'During the show, there is a hanging sequence, a baby is torn apart, a mother sliced down the middle, and a beautiful girl has her throat cut. At the climax of the one-and-a-half-hour performance, young fans in the front rows are soaked by gallons of theatrical blood'. Blunkett, in fact, couldn't have seen anything because he is blind, but this is beside the point. He probably never attended the show and was relying on reports that were fed back to him. The only exaggeration is the 'gallons of blood', though Funaro had had more than enough of it: 'We could not get the smell of cherry juice off us for days. The poor wardrobe lady had her hands full. I was more interested in keeping the groove together. Theatrics are the foundation of Alice's show. The more enhanced, the better the reaction from the audience. There were still a few of us that actually cared what was going on musically'.

Stockholm (16 April) saw 'He's Back' appear in the encore. This one-off appearance was due to it reaching number 4 on the Swedish singles chart in 1986. If the audience loved it, Mary wasn't so sure: 'We couldn't really leave it out, but it was a song that didn't seem to fit in that great musically with what we were doing'.

Meanwhile, the authorities in West Germany were clamping down on the show, with the reaction being worse than in the UK. Alice recounted an amusing example to *Metal Hammer* (July 1989): 'These guys in Bavaria kept going on about these dolls that I used in my show. They had believed the exaggerated claims of an unnamed sensationalist daily paper; they were that stupid. Whatever, I wasn't under any circumstances allowed to use the dolls on stage. So I asked whether I could use teddy bears instead – NO TEDDY BEARS! An honest answer and the press had a field day the following morning. At the concert that evening, hundreds of kids who had read in the paper that Alice Cooper wasn't allowed to use teddy bears, chucked them on stage'.

Mary says: 'They were telling the management company you can't kill babies onstage. Like yeah, of course you can't! Somehow the rumour ended up being bigger than the actual show. When we played Munich, they didn't allow anyone under the age of eighteen to go. There was a dome and they had armed guards with machine guns all round the perimeter of the dome. I remember thinking, 'yeah, this is a little odd'.' Kane adds that 'In Munich, if Alice put the baby's head on the end of the sword, they were going to shut the show down'.

Kane's take on the show is that 'It was definitely a culture of violence. There's a scene, I think it was 'Gail', and there's a prostitute on stage. Alice comes out of the darkness with a huge blade and he goes up to her. He's about to stab her and he stops, looking at the audience, suggesting, 'should I?' Of course, the crowd would go crazy, 'Yes!' It was like that everywhere except Italy. The same scene takes place, but the audience suddenly gets quiet. He lifts the knife over her head and looks at the audience and they said, 'No!' It turned into this whole deal. So Alice does it like three times and then he slits her throat, blood flying all over the place and a riot breaks out. Some guys get on stage, pulling some of the crew into the audience. It went absolutely crazy'. With only a couple more dates to go before the end of the tour, there were no changes made. But the Italian reaction highlighted some of the misgivings Epic Records (then negotiating with Alice) had about continuing in the same direction.

Funaro was still hanging on in there: 'I occasionally had to reach way down deep to find a reason to be there besides the money. I could smoke and drink on stage so that was a big plus! However, I was thoroughly entertained whenever one of the mechanical pieces would fail. Alice is a pro, and he recovered like one all the time. But sometimes, I couldn't keep from laughing. Especially when Alice would make 'Jerry Lewis' faces at me when he came up the stairs when no one else could see. I did lose my shit and busted out laughing on the last show of the second tour (6 May, Forest National, Brussels). He made the most amazing face, cross-eyed and just full of distorted reality. I left that gig truly loving Alice as a performer and as a bandmate. He was never insecure or jealous of anyone. Good man; good boss'.

As the tour ended, plans were being made for the next move. Other than Kane, the band were all off in other directions. Taylor knew he was leaving at the tour's end to hook up with Kip. He would be back again and left on good terms: 'I learned that you go out there and have a great time, but you turn up on time and you're respectful. He is just a great guy. The stories are endless. A superstar and class act'. Kane's opinion is that 'I don't think anyone was super-disappointed. Kip was on his way to something else. Stylistically Ken wanted to go somewhere else. That's what happens'.

However, it seems that Alice could possibly have kept the phenomenal Ken Mary onside if things had been different: 'With me personally, I had made the choice to leave. I love Shep, I love Alice and generally speaking, it was a kind organisation. Shep is awesome and I would have loved to have a manager like Shep for my whole career. That being said, there were a couple of people in the organisation that are no longer there that were very difficult to deal with. They made you feel that 'You know you need to go so get yourself something else happening; don't think of this as home'. I feel they were unnecessarily flippant about the contributions of the band as well. Maybe someone should have pulled

Alice and Shep aside to let them know what was going on with these other people. We were young and I would handle it differently nowadays. Back then, I was like, OK, I guess I'd better get a different gig going, so that's why I left. But you know it wasn't a bad split; it was amicable and there was no dissatisfaction. But yes, I would have stayed with Alice but not under the circumstances there were with some of the people in the organisation. To sum it all up, it really was a fantastic experience that I would not trade. Also, the audiences were special; they were there to have a great time. They were just going nuts the entire time'.

In The Flesh Dress Rehearsals (DVD)

The only decent document of the tour is the footage that can be found on the Extras disc of the *Prime Cuts* release. It's scattered through the disc but can be easiest found by going straight to Chapter two and fast-forwarding. It's professionally filmed with lots of close-ups and the sound is excellent. In order, you will find: 'I'm Eighteen', 'Dead Babies', 'Killer', 'School's Out', 'Billion Dollar Babies', 'No More Mr. Nice Guy' and 'Only Women Bleed'.

1989 – Trash

Trash (Epic)

Personnel:

Alice Cooper: vocals

John McCurry: guitar

Alan St. Jon: keyboards, backing vocals

Hugh McDonald: bass, backing vocals

Bobby Chouinard: drums

With:

Paul Chiten: keyboards

Steve Deutsch: synth programming

Gregg Mangiafico: keyboards, special effects

Guy Mann-Dude: guitar on 'Spark In The Dark', 'Why Trust You', 'This Maniac's in Love With You' and the intro to 'Bed Of Nails'

Joe Perry: guitar on 'House Of Fire'

Steven Tyler: additional lead vocals on 'Only My Heart Talkin''

Kane Roberts: guitar on 'Bed Of Nails'

Jon Bon Jovi: additional lead vocals on 'Trash'

Mark Frazier & Jack Johnson: guitars on 'Trash'

Tom Hamilton: bass on 'Trash'

Joey Kramer: drums on 'Trash'

Steve Lukather & Richie Sambora: guitars on 'Hell Is Living Without You'

Kip Winger: backing vocals on 'I'm Your Gun'

Tom Teeley: backing vocals on 'This Maniac's In Love With You' and others

Joe Turano: backing vocals on 'Bed Of Nails' and others

Jamie Sever: backing vocals on 'Trash'

(Rouge) Diana Graselli, Myriam Valle, Maria Vidal: backing vocals

Michael Anthony, Stiv Bators, Desmond Child, Jango, Louie Merlino, Bernie Shanahan: backing vocals

Produced at Bearsville Studios, The Power Station, Right Track, Sigma Sound Studios, Mediasound, Grog Kill Studios, Village Recorders, The Complex, Record Plant, Blue Jay Studios and Sanctuary Sound, May – June 1989 by Desmond Child

Release date: 25 July 1989

Highest chart places: UK: 2, USA: 20

Running time: 40:11

During the *In the Flesh* tour Bob Pfeiffer, A&R at Epic Records, approached Alice and Shep with an offer to sign with Epic. When the duo realised the extent that Epic were prepared to go to to get Alice they signed right away. They could do whatever it took to make a successful album and they could have the currently hot Desmond Child as producer.

The touring band moved on, except for Kane, who stuck with Alice until August 1988, at which point he took a solo deal. Kane recalls 'What happened was we had had another gun guitar made for me. Then I got a record deal on Geffen and Alice hooked up with Desmond. Then Desmond and I started writing together. So it turned into a thing that if I was going to give Alice Cooper proper attention, I would have to not do my album. Also, the people Alice was with now wanted a stylistic change'.

Kane and Alice 'parted' on good terms and have worked together since. Kane still laughs at their big 'split': 'He would often stop at mine when he was in California. When the decision came that I wasn't in the band anymore, Alice was knocking at my door first thing in the morning. He was holding two suitcases and he goes, 'I'm leaving you'. He made it like some romantic drama'.

May to June saw Alice putting *Trash* together in more studios for one album than he had ever done before. He clearly relished the prospects: 'Being on a new label is unbelievable. MCA didn't have any idea about me, Epic is great, though', he told *Raw* (May 1989). So why had Alice selected Child? 'The only time I turn up the radio is when something really kills me, which means that my radio's down most of the time! Anyway, I'm driving in the Corvette and I heard 'Dude (Looks Like A Lady)' and I thought, 'what a great song; the best thing I've heard in years'. Next, I heard that Bon Jovi song 'Livin' On A Prayer'. Another one I liked was Kiss' 'Heaven's On Fire'. So I asked Brian (Renfield) to find out who did all this. When he told me it was Desmond Child, I thought, 'Wow, I've gotta work with this guy because he's writing the sort of music I wanna hear'. Combine my input and voice with that style gives you the album I'd wanna make for the 1990s'.

Going for Desmond Child was not without risks. One thing he didn't have was a pedigree of producing records. He had co-produced many, but only one, Bonnie Tyler's *Hide Your Heart* (1988), bore his name alone. It's likely there were nerves about that from the Cooper camp, as well as who would be playing on the record. Guitarist John McCurry touches on that: 'I remember Desmond saying, 'We're going to be doing some demos with Alice Cooper'. He was aware that Alice didn't want to have some studio cats doing his next record. When we met Alice, we were in a rehearsal studio, SIR or somewhere. He wanted to see who we were and get to know us. We had some potential songs that Desmond was working on so Alice could listen to the band play. After we played, Desmond introduced us to Alice. He introduced me first: 'John McCurry's toured with this one and that one; he doesn't read any music at all'. Alice said, 'So what, is that good?' Desmond was trying to impress upon him that I was flying by the seat of my pants and I wasn't a session cat. Bobby Chouinard was as far from a session cat as one could get. Hugh McDonald was quietly working with Bon Jovi'.

Alice was reassured by the meeting and plans went ahead for what McCurry agrees was, 'A Desmond Child package' with an Alice spin on it and several guests. Amazingly the only constants on every track are Alice and Desmond Child.

The thought of writing with Desmond thrilled Alice. 'When Desmond and I were writing, we were listening to *Love It To Death* and the *Greatest Hits* LPs. Not because I wanted to throw back to that, just to find that vibe and match it to the present era. (*Kerrang*, August 1989). Then again, he said to *The Music Page* in November 1989: 'When I did *Billion Dollar Babies* or *School's Out*, we were really writing songs, and that's what I wanted to do. Desmond is excellent at writing songs. He's terrific in that sense. You can hear the difference right away. With the last album, we didn't really spend time writing the songs as we should have done'.

The title and concept came from Alice: 'Trash is the word I use for everything that excites me. Trash is the girl with an amazing body that walks past me on Sunset Boulevard; Trash is the fantastic feeling I get behind the steering wheel of a fast car while zooming down the highway; Trash is sensational and impressive, *Trash* is the best possible title for the album, and I think this LP is the best Alice Cooper had recorded in ages'. (*Metal Hammer*, July 1989)

Alice admitted that 'It was also really important for me to include tracks that can be played on the radio. I mean, I'm not stupid; I know exactly what I have to do to get my music more airplay than I got during the *Constrictor* and *Raise Your Fist* times. So I wrote the songs accordingly'. (*Metal Hammer*, July 1989)

A common complaint about the album is that it sounds strongly like a Desmond Child record with Alice guesting on it. We don't get anything like the full range and diversity Alice is capable of. Gregg Mangiafico (keyboards) stresses that the intention positively *was* to bring out the

'Alice' personality: 'Part of Desmond's job was to channel Alice. He has a huge gift to become the artist he is working with so that he knows what that artist needs. My memory of the sessions was that he and Alice were in complete synch'.

One whose 'personality' is not submerged is Joan Jett's. She comes through in spades on 'House Of Fire', even though she doesn't sing on it. She wrote most or all of it and it sounds *exactly* like a Jett song. It stands out from the Child formula because of that. Similarly, the other best tracks are 'This Maniac's In Love With You', 'Trash' and 'I'm Your Gun' – all of which offer snap, crackle and less pop. Keyboards player Alan St. Jon says they knew the old fanbase might find *Trash* hard to love: 'It's a very smart produced album that is different to Alice's previous work, which is possibly why his hardcore fans had a hard time digesting it'.

McCurry used to tease Child about his formula: 'I said, 'Desmond, why don't you use some different chords, instead of 'Living On A Prayer' for everything?', and he said, 'Why mess with a good thing? I'm stealing from myself!''

Many of the musicians had little knowledge of Alice's back catalogue. This didn't phase him, as McCurry recounts: 'He looked at me once in the studio and said, 'You don't know any of my old songs, do you?' I said, 'I'm Eighteen', and he said 'Yeah, what else?' I said, ''School's Out'; I don't know any more, I can't lie'. He said, 'Well, don't; I had you figured out anyway; I still like you'. He's such a sweet guy, the nicest guy I've ever worked with'.

Twenty tracks were recorded for the album and the best ten were picked. Only one of the three songs Jon Bon Jovi penned was used, and similarly, only one of three by Kane Roberts. The core of the musicians came from Billy Squier's band. Bobby Chouinard was Squier's drummer and was recommended by McCurry: 'He needed a gig and he was a great rock 'n' roll drummer, but he wasn't very flexible, either as a person or stylistically. The funniest thing I saw was Desmond jumping up and down in front of Bobby, trying to get Bobby inspired to pick up the tempo. Bobby would just say, 'No!' He would not look at him. Bobby Chouinard could play at one tempo all day and all night long. He had a remarkable groove and he added a rock credibility to some of Desmond's records'.

Alan St. Jon came in on keyboards: 'Shep called and he said he wants a band in, so he wanted most of the Squier band. Bobby and I were best friends. He was compared a lot to John Bonham and he was just as good in my head. For bass, they got Hugh McDonald, who had been playing live with Bon Jovi but had done bass parts on their records. My actual real name is Levi, but Squier and I thought when I did radio interviews, they would mispronounce it. So Billy said, 'From now on, you're St. Jon (with no H)'. The H was put in by mistake on the Trash credits. Desmond brought a sense of musicality to Alice's career, which Alice had not been recognised for. He was more of a theatrical artist, so when we went in with him, it was a question of how we would approach the project'.

Mangiafico also felt the Child/Cooper link-up was a perfect match: 'Alice is known for the horror and the shock. When you work with Alice, he will tell you what he might like you to play, but he won't say, 'I don't like that', he will say, 'It's not right for Alice'. I think Desmond and Alice were a great fit'.

Child's regular team of backing vocalists were added into the mix, including Rouge (Diana Grasselli, Myrian Valle and Maria Vidal), who he had cut two excellent albums with in their own right. Grasselli details how they worked on *Trash*: 'The way it worked in the studio there were some big groups of vocalists and we all had certain parts that we were singing. Those are the big choral background things that you are hearing and they are often multi-tracked, a sort of wall of voices. When it came to some of the other tracks, we might have five singers and they would be specially picked chosen voices that worked well together. When you're singing background parts, there's a set of skills. You work with your ears and your voice to make your voice combine with other voices to sound like one voice. The vocals on the tracks that I/we sang on, particularly 'Poison', 'Bed Of Nails' and 'Hell is Living Without You', were orchestral/choral and really spiritual. Those vocals are very special on this record'.

Grasselli enjoyed working with Alice: 'He is amazing, so normal and down to earth. He was there all the time and he had suggestions. I remember he definitely had opinions about the feel on things. You know, 'It's too sweet, it needs to be tougher', mostly to do with textures'. She also identified one mystery backing singer credited as Michael Anthony. 'He was Michael Anthony Rodriguez. He was one of Desmond's production assistants and a singer. He was also Dianne Warren's right-hand person'.

Special guests were brought in to add colour and their appearance added to the sense that this was a special album. Alice never needs much prompting to talk about guitarists, telling *Guitar* in February 1990 that: 'John McCurry was a friend who played guitar on the basic tracks. Then we had a feast of guitar players – Steve Lukather, Richie Sambora, Joe Perry – which was great because I'm a guitar addict'. McCurry's role is underplayed there. His work on the album is outstanding. As he says, "'Poison' and 'I'm Your Gun' are definitely all me guitar-wise'.

One guitarist Alice oddly didn't mention was Guy Mann-Dude, whose flair and panache lights up several tracks. Mann-Dude was 'Recording my first album *Sleight Of Hand,* for MCA at Village Recorders in Los Angeles. Alice was recording there, too and needed some guitar work. Through my producer, and other people at the studio, Alice found out about me. A week or so later, I was in the control room and turned around to find Alice standing right behind me! I was taken aback. We just kind of shot the shit, real friendly. We didn't talk about music or him needing guitar work done or anything like that. I think he just wanted to see what I was like'.

'A few days later, I was told to go see Alice over at his studio. Alice and Desmond Child were there. Alice asked me to listen to three songs. Well, I'm listening and I'm thinking to myself, 'What the fuck, this is Alice Cooper and these songs sound like John Cougar!' At the time, I didn't know who Desmond Child was and didn't care, I had to be real and so when the last song ended, I point blankly said to everyone, 'These songs need some heavy guitar here to make it more heavy metal'. I thought they were gonna throw me out of the studio, but to my surprise, Alice stood up and said, 'He's right, it needs to be more heavy metal'.

'A few days later, I got called in to work on these tunes. I did three full days of re-doing rhythms and solos. I had free rein to do what I wanted. I spent long hours on them too! I wanted to get some good work done. I wasn't paid a fucking dime for all my work, but Alice did do a vocal thing (a count-in) on 'On The Verge' for my *Sleight Of Hand* album. It was good press, so everyone figured it was a trade-off'.

'Most of the guitar work I did was on my own, but there were a few times Desmond suggested something and I gladly tried what he would tell me. He was brilliant, easy and fun to work with. We got along well, and after *Trash* was finished, he asked me to co-write a few songs for the movie soundtrack *Shocker*'.

Mann-Dude was living the dream: 'Working with Alice was a breeze. I flew with Desmond from LA to Chicago and we picked up Alice and his wife there. We then flew to New York and all of us rode in a limousine to Woodstock, New York, to Bearsville Studio. I enjoyed Alice's stories about him drinking with Jim Morrison and such. It was definitely fun riding in a limo for two hours with Alice!'

The album's basic tracks were laid down at Power Station in New York and Bearsville Studios in Woodstock. Who plays what and where on the record is possible to sort out, with one exception – keyboards/ synths. Four men are credited, with St. Jon clearly in the main position: 'Desmond and I got along great. He was a sweet man to work with. Anything that's black and white I play; keyboards, piano, the lot, plus backing vocals. If Alice or Desmond had a sound or idea in their head, they would come up to me and I would grab it. Paul Chiten, Gregg Mangiafico and Steve Deutsch were probably doing the more technical stuff that I just had no patience for. I am not opposed to using synths, but if it's not the right sound for the song, then why use it? All those high harmony vocals were like tripled, quadrupled, quintupled track-wise'.

Mangiafico feels that the reason for so many keyboard players was because 'All of us in those days were busy, or maybe it was down to style choices. The phone would ring and you would go do it'. He was there at the Bearsville sessions in particular: 'As well as overdubs, I played regular keyboard parts too. When we did the live tracking days, Desmond usually liked the keyboard player to do what he called the big sound. So it would be DX7 with electric pianos, harpsichords, and then some big Oberheim-type pads. Just a real stacked midi sound. It had a percussive edge to it and it also had a big string organ swell to it. We were there for four or five days at Bearsville doing two or three basic tracks a day. Overdubs might be going on in another room. I know I did some overdubs, too, where I was thickening up on some keyboards that had already been recorded. Maybe playing a sympathetic add-on part. When we were doing the organ things, we had to go to Carla Bley's studio (Grog Kill) because Bearsville was booked out. For those sessions, it was just me, Desmond, Alice and the engineer Arthur Payson. We worked till two or four in the morning, putting in some pretty serious hours. Desmond often had an idea of what he wanted, he would sing you a part and you would fill in the rest of it'.

Child was a busy man at Bearsville, where he was recording two acts at the same time. Mangiafico recalls that: 'You could be playing with Robin Beck in one room and Alice Cooper in the other room. Guy played on both of those too'. The Robin Beck album, *Trouble Or Nothin'*, features a host of the *Trash* players, with Child producing and also writing or co-writing five songs, including 'Hold Back The Night' with Alice.

Mangiafico worked on some fascinating overdubs at Bearsville: 'Not all of them got used. I got a theatre organ sound on the keyboards and made up these horror movie cue things, like the Bach D-Minor organ. Alice was going to put one between each of the songs, but most never made it onto the album. My understanding was that they weren't intended to be part of a song'. Two of those cues, for 'Poison' and 'Bed Of Nails', did make it onto the finished record but were incorporated into the songs.

Paul Chiten (synthesiser) first met Desmond Child earlier in 1989 for the Music Speaks Louder Than Words songwriters summit: 'A group of about thirty really good Los Angeles-based songwriters went to Moscow to write with our Russian counterparts. An album was released on Epic Records of the twelve best songs that came out of the trip. Desmond Child was on that trip so we became friendly. I am a piano player, and wherever we sat and there was a piano, I would play. So he heard me play every day and he said, 'When we get back to LA, I want you to come to play on the album', so I said, 'Great'.' Chiten concurs with Mangiafico that Child was bringing in the best of who was available and was after different styles: 'There are lots of reasons why Desmond would have used four keyboard players – 1. Who is available, 2. Is the studio time going to be available when they are available, 3. Different people have different styles; one guy might be best for jazz or rock or blues. So you bring in different people for different flavours'.

Chiten played on afternoon overdub sessions at Village Recorders in Hollywood. 'In the end, I actually played synthesisers on the album, I don't think I did a piano track. I don't think I'm on every track, either. The basic track would be done and then I would add synthesiser. A lot of the track would be finished, almost ready for the final mix. The two of us sat in the control room. I had my synthesisers there because it was easier than being out in the main room. Desmond would say, 'Give me something like this', and I would play something bluesy, for example. We worked well together and I really liked him. Alice was there at some point, but I didn't interact with him. Sometimes your part is featured and pushed up in the mix, but sometimes it's down in the background. Every song is different and demands something different. I worked to guide vocals, lead lines or lines that answer the vocal. What I did could be anything from pads to holding a chord which would be used in the back of a track'.

It wasn't all hard work on the album. Grasselli recalls a trip out together: 'The studio went down with some kind of technical problem. Alice loved movies and said, 'OK, let's go to the movies'. So we all piled into the car and we went to the Mall. We arrived and there's a long line of teenagers and he said, 'Oh, it's Saturday. I forgot! OK, Diana, you walk right in front of me. Everybody else, you just surround me, don't let anybody see me'. We walk towards the line of people and of course, one guy saw him, saying, 'Ah, you're Alice Cooper!', so Alice looked at him and said, 'Ssshhh'. Then we all ran like hell into the cinema. It was so funny'.

The cover finished off the glossy package in style, although it looks like it was selected by a committee to hit the right spot. It's a slick image of Alice that played safe and one that dismayed Ernie Cefalu of Pacific Eye & Ear: 'We had done something for *Trash,* but Shep wasn't happy with it, so they used somebody else. They did that ugly jacket'.

Trash was the huge smash it was hoped to be. St Jon sums it up: 'You can tell what stamp Alice has put on each of the songs. He knew what he wanted. I think Alice is really proud of the *Trash* album. It brought him back in people's eyes'.

Mangiafico is similarly enthused: 'I was thankful to be on it. Those key changes are amazing; there was nobody else doing that kind of thing. The bridge, the verse and the chorus would all be in different keys; the songs felt good'.

Chiten knew this was going to be a big record. 'Sometimes you get a feeling and I had that about this album. Wonderful songs inspired performances and Alice's vocals were good. Everything just worked'.

Grasselli was 'glad' to finish the album: 'You might sing something literally like 35 times. So after you are done with the gig, you are like, 'Oh God, I don't wanna hear that again!' Then after a while, you go back, listen and go, 'That's really good!' After we finished the album, I got a plane to France. I jumped in a taxi and, as it was going down the main drag, I heard 'Poison' coming out of a store. I thought, 'Oh my God, I can't get away from it!' That's how it was the whole summer, it was just played everywhere!'

When Alice came out with his next album, *Hey Stoopid*, he was asked by *Metal Forces* (July 1991) if, in retrospect, he thought that *Trash* was too soft and too commercial: 'In the studio, Desmond Child is a very overpowering force. You don't realise that until you sit down and really listen to the record. There was too much Desmond on *Trash* and not enough Alice. Although I do think that the biggest hit single, 'Poison', was a real Alice song. Whereas 'Bed Of Nails' and 'House Of Fire' were a bit too Desmond'.

'Poison' (Cooper/ Child/ McCurry)

Alan St, Jon says that, 'The first track we recorded was 'Poison'. The strongest song they felt and they wanted to get it out there. John (McCurry) had that great riff for Alice. We knew it was going to be a big song as soon as we started work on it'.

Alice recalled that: 'The riff in 'Poison' didn't come along until the very end' (*RIP*, September 1990), while McCurry feels that they had the riff first. That would seem to be the likeliest scenario, given that the riff pre-dated the album sessions. McCurry had written and recorded it two years earlier with John Waite for his song 'Encircled'. He recalls that: 'Alice said, 'I'm looking for something that sounds like Guns 'N' Roses' 'Sweet Child O' Mine''. So I said I have this that I've done years ago for John. I think they worked something out with John for using it. We did it in a different key and a different tempo. 'Poison' is in the key of D and John's was in E'.

One thing that Alice queried was McCurry's guitar: 'I used a Fender parts guitar, a Frankenstein guitar. Alice asked me where my Gibsons were, 'You're gonna play a Strat on my thing?!' 'I said, 'Yeah, you should hear it', but Alice says, 'That sounds great; I was teasing you'.

Alice knew he had the lead-off single: 'When it comes to a single, you pick the strongest material. 'Poison' was so unique, I think, that it was almost like we didn't pick it. When the album came out, 'Poison' was on the radio so fast and on so many stations that it was making our heads spin. It more or less fell off the album' (*Scene*, March 1990).

It is the strongest track on the album in one particular way, representing the best outcome of the project, whereby Alice adds his own 'spin' onto the Desmond Child formula. It was a fresh sound for Alice that he portrayed well, using the character to sell the song. Nothing else on the album comes as close as this to making the project work, but there are other better songs that do not quite fit the formula.

It opens with a synthesiser 'pow', an overdub c/o Mangiafico, that grabs the attention: 'That's one of mine. I did a lot of advertising work, so as a synthesiser player for that, you have to do a lot of whooshing and swooshing. The basic sound there came out of the sampler I was using at the time'. The synth leads right into the famous riff. McCurry

128

notes that: 'I always got the sense that they took my guitar's feedback at the beginning and turned it around. I just came in with a long swell on the guitar, hit the strings and swelled my volume up'.

It's obvious as soon as the rhythm section falls in behind McCurry that we have a more polished Alice. They delay Alice's entry until 38 seconds have elapsed, long enough to convey a sense of the star arrival. He sounds instantly more assured and more convincingly Alice than he has for many years. It's a sensual vocal with Alice teasing the listener and enticing us in. Cleverly they don't head straight into the chorus but allow verse two to build the pressure and a head of steam – 'I want to love you, but I better not touch'. It's on this verse that you're struck by the wall of sound backing vocalists and keyboards. St. Jon explains his role on the song as 'Coming up with sound textures, soundscaping the song'.

By the time we hit the first chorus, everything is immense, with Alice now at the top of his range. It's hugely impressive and the chorus is as big as it needed to be. McCurry says that Desmond, 'Was very proud of the fact that from the verse to the chorus, the song modulates four or five times. There was a massive group singing the ah's; there must have been thirty people out there'. Grasselli says, 'That's one of those situations where there was a group singing that was multi-tracked, and then there was a group session where all of us would sing at once. Then all of that was mixed together. 'Poison' is my absolute favourite Alice song because of the chord structure, the melody, and the way it takes off in twists and turns. Those huge releases in the melodies and harmonies are just gorgeous'. St. Jon is also one of the backing vocalists: 'Vocally, it just kicked my ass because the hook is so strong. I mean, he'd never done a song before that'd had that modulation in it. It was pretty interesting watching that one develop'.

The same formula is repeated for another sensual verse, followed by the big build-up through the next verse ('I Hear you calling and it's needles and pins'), into the chorus. After the chorus, a teasing fill from McCurry hints at the solo to come and then straight back into another verse/chorus. From 3:30, it's wave after wave of choruses with McCurry on stunning form: 'I love the solo; we worked together on it. Alice really liked that sneaky intro thing I do with the tremolo bar. Desmond said, 'What is that? It sounds like crap. I don't want that'. Alice said, 'We're keeping it". They should have mixed McCurry's guitar up louder. It won't be the last time the guitars aren't mixed right, but it's the most criminal example.

It is a classic Alice song, but a little dirt and grime would have helped offset the gloss and the polish.

An eye-popping video was recorded for 'Poison' which helped propel it to a heady number two in the UK, kept off the top spot by Jive Bunny and The Master Mixers' 'Swing The Mood'. It also went top ten in America, reaching number 7.

'Spark In The Dark' (Cooper/ Child)

This could have been so much better. It's a big step down from the heights of 'Poison' and lacks energy. The wandering guitar riff, however, is absolutely terrific and should have been dialled right up with the keyboards turned down. There is a really good rock song submerged in the mix if they had decided to rock it out more to remove some of the bland gloss. This is one where style wins out over substance.

'House Of Fire' (Cooper/ Child/ Joan Jett)

The song was originally written by Child and Jett to go on her 1988 album *Up Your Alley*. Jett felt it was more suited to Bon Jovi, so Child passed it to them. They demoed it for *New Jersey*, but also passed on it for the final cut, though it has been subsequently issued on the deluxe edition. The next stop was Alice, as Child felt it could work well for *Trash*.

Quite what Alice added to the songwriting is uncertain as it's pure Joan Jett, but he must have added or altered one or two lines.

What the song needed was Joan Jett herself. She would have kept things a little rougher and dirtier, more rock 'n' roll. They should have begged her to add her own distinctive rhythm playing to the track and maybe got her to duet as well.

The glitter stomping intro sees Joe Perry adding the requisite fire. Nobody was turning him down and it's good to hear the guitars cranked up. The dumb simplicity of it all works a treat. It still has the multiple backing vocals, but they work well, and when Perry solos, you can't help but smile with pleasure. Notice, though, the sheer number of guitars on the track. Quite often, you can hear another guitar blazing away low in the mix and there are who knows how many rhythm parts. One of them is certainly McCurry: 'I played rhythm guitar on that, but I didn't finish it; I don't remember overdubbing on it'. St. Jon says it was one of the more challenging ones because 'On the more metal tracks, it's hard for a keyboard player to find the right approach'.

It's not a great track, but there is a joy and warmth to it that's hard to resist. It was released as the third single from the album.

'Why Trust You' (Cooper/ Child)

Mann-Dude says. 'The first song I recorded was 'Why Trust You' and there were about a dozen people in the studio! Record execs and such checking me out. I killed it and ripped the solo for everyone to see! I had already laid down the rhythm tracks'.

In tone and feel, it's 'Spark In The Dark' part two, but there are some positives that stand out. Mann-Dude's shredding guitar fills keep things lively and Alice turns in a spirited vocal, getting in a range of vocal inflections. The line (at 0:41), 'You're a psychopathic liar, your soul is on fire, you're bluffin' with nothin', while the stakes are gettin' higher' is his most frenetic delivery yet on the album. He repeats the delivery twice more in the song but with different lyrics, although equally as damning.

Apart from a few fills, Mann-Dude is restricted to a chugging rhythm guitar part until 1:56, when he rips out the expected solo. He doesn't let us down, with a torrent of notes squealing out of his guitar in a vibrant, colourful solo. The a capella solo Alice vocal ending is good too, but overall there's a sense that this could have been a better song if it had been rougher and dirtier.

'Only My Heart Talkin' (Cooper/ Bruce Roberts/ Andy Goldmark)

Alice said to *Metal Hammer* in July 1989: 'Des and I listened to the tape one day, coming to the joint opinion that a song like that was really missing from the album. The only thing that disturbed me were the lyrics. They weren't my style; they weren't what I would have normally said and sung. So we reworked the track. Desmond tackled the musical side, changing the arrangements and I worked over the lyrics on numerous occasions'.

Andy Goldmark, who wrote it with Bruce Roberts, recalled that: 'I gave it to Desmond Child, who I've known a long time. He liked it and played it for Alice, who felt the same way. In its basic form, the song and the demo are more pop than anything. Desmond rocked it up quite a bit with big guitars and drums, which made it work really well for Alice. Instead of the simple, intimate keyboard/drum machine approach in the demo, it came back blown out stadium-ready'.

McCurry says: 'That was sort of Stones meets Axl style. It wasn't as many parts as 'Poison', but I came up with all those sliding-around parts. I structured the verse parts. I also play an acoustic on it'.

It was also a song that St. Jon got a chance to flex his muscles on: 'I did a bunch of stuff on there orchestration-wise. It was a song that was very outside of Alice's wheelhouse. It was my first chance to really stretch out on the keyboards on the album. I also did backing vocals and they were a lot of fun to record'. On the other hand, Gregg Mangiafico feels the string parts might be his work: 'The really cool string part sounds like one of mine. When Desmond wanted that, he would call for a Paul Buckmaster style, the man who did strings for Elton'.

The stadium-friendly power ballad style was a new area for Alice, but it had served the likes of Heart and Aerosmith well. Speaking of Steven Tyler, Alice told *Circus* in 1989 that: 'I called Steven, who loved the song, so we went to Boston, sat in the studio for about eight hours and had fun. I sang as high as I possibly could, and he was up there, even higher. That's one vocal I would not want to have to do again'.

The song was the kind that might well appeal to casual record buyers. Epic didn't push it as a single in all territories, and on a quality, rather than saturation, level, at least they were justified because the song is pretty pedestrian bar a few brief glimmers of interest.

The duet itself is pointless. While Tyler's presence evokes Aerosmith's 'I Don't Wanna Miss A Thing', that's all it does. 'Only My Heart Talkin'' is nowhere near as effective as that song, though similarly, the orchestration is one of the best things here.

There's a lot going on in the backing tracks with Alice on top form with his breathy unguarded and honest delivery. Where it goes wrong is the dull chorus, which doesn't soar out over the verses. The best part is McCurry's brief, lovely melodic solo at 2:31. He's back again at 3:43 with some textures and fills that could have done with mixing louder.

The obviously missed trick was not making it a duet with a female vocalist. That would have to wait till late in the *Trash* tour when Devon Meade got her chance in the spotlight. The song was released as the fourth single from *Trash* in some markets.

'Bed Of Nails' (Cooper/ Child/ Kane Roberts/ Dianne Warren)
Side two on the vinyl opens with this 'sequel' to 'Poison'. The 'concept', such as it is, was a simple one. Alice explained to *Guitar* (February 1990) that he got started on it after wondering, 'What would Alice do with a sadistic female lover? Would he be a sadistic lover also?'

Everything is set up for this to be one of the big bangers on the album but it could have been better. For St. Jon, it was a definite highlight:

'That was a great song; I used a Roland Jupiter 8 keyboard on that. It's a ballad, well close to a ballad, so I wanted a combination of sounds knitted together, which would be strings, piano and whatever little tinkly sounds came to mind. It was a huge vocal effort too'.

The intro is the uncredited Guy Mann-Dude playing the 'Poison' riff slowly, which is a brilliant link back to that track. Guy says that it was 'A short overdub. For some reason, they wanted a reprise of 'Poison', so I play the riff really slow at the very beginning. I did this at Woodstock at Bearsville Studio'.

Low in the mix on the intro is a horror film-style keyboard part (a la 'Gail'), courtesy of Mangiafico, that could have done with more prominence. From there, it's a gallop of drums and guitars into the first verse. Lyrically it's fluff and nonsense, a bit obvious, sanitised and dull.

Paul Chiten says, 'I recognised my playing, particularly on the passage from 2:55 to 3:10. There's a keyboard pad that sounds like voices, which was one of my signature sounds at the time'. McCurry plays the rhythm parts on the song and works on the arrangement, which he 'helped to sketch out'.

The song is salvaged by Kane Roberts, who gets some attack and bite into the lead guitar, especially on his solo at 2:42. Kane says, 'I wanted to do a solo that reflected his voice, instead of a super shred solo. I did some rhythm parts on it, but most of it is John McCurry, who is one of the best rhythm guys you could have'. McCurry and Roberts became firm friends from then on. McCurry says that 'Kane's feelings were hurt that he wasn't part of this record. Once when we were hangin' he said, 'You know I wanted to kill you?' I said, 'Excuse me?', and he said, 'Well, you took my gig'. Of course, I didn't know any of the history. I played on Kane's record'.

The other redeeming feature is the chorus which is Child and Dianne Warren at their best. The hook is fabulous and the wall of sound backing vocals are stunning, with Alice in better form than on the verses. Among the backing vocalists was Joe Turano: 'I was doing a wide range of vocal sessions in those days. I recall it being in the evening and Alice was not there. I always loved working with Desmond. He was an exacting producer, at least as far as vocals were concerned, so I enjoyed the challenge. I may have multi-tracked my own voice or possibly sung with Desmond. He liked to stack lots of vocal tracks. Desmond called me in after vocals were already cut to add my voice to the equation. I have a high, distinctive voice that can have a raspy quality, and he liked the texture it added'.

From 3:09 onwards, Kane plays off Alice as they smash out chorus after chorus. Kane plays some great licks all the way to the outro. It was released as the second single off the album.

'This Maniac's In Love With You (Cooper/ Child/ Bob Held/ Tom Teeley)
Alice told *Raw* (July 1989) that it was 'a song that does go back a little to Alice's horror thing. It's almost like this guy is stalking someone; he loves them so much he's possessed by them'. Alice was spot-on here because, at last, you can really hear Alice wound up and revelling in being Alice.

Mann-Dude is terrific, too, with some exciting, vibrant guitar, although he remains unhappy about how they used his solo: 'Desmond had the stupid idea of using a solo that was already there and mine that I worked hard on! I was pissed about that! I thought it was a lame idea! The un-metalness came out of Desmond on that one. So all the rhythm guitar parts and licks are mine but on the solo, you mostly hear mine on the left side; John McCurry is on the right'.

It's a simple track that motors along on rhythm guitar, bass, drums and cowbell, with Mann-Dude throwing shapes over the top. The verses with Alice leaving gaps between the lines are great and the catchy chorus doesn't disappoint.

As the choruses roll on, there's a neat backing vocal at 3:14 that copies the descending riff that Mann-Dude uses to great effect. This song is a welcome shot of excitement, with an energised Mann-Dude killing the guitar.

The genesis of the song was a demo by Bob Held and Tom Teeley. Held played bass on the demo, while Teeley sang, playing guitar and synth. It's terrific, with Teeley's edgy high vocal fitting the lyrics perfectly. Teeley says, 'I really got off on how high I sang. I thought the riff was almost Hendrix-y. I sang along with it and doubled it with the guitar'.

The completed demo, in the key of A, was passed by Held to his publisher, Don Glearson, who was A&Ring at Epic Records. Held says, 'Don then gave it to Desmond Child. Then Desmond hired Tom for the vocal arrangements and he also did background vocals. Teeley was there, 'For about two weeks. I sang on the whole record with a small team of vocalists, it was fun, I had a great time'.

While Teeley was recording vocals for 'This Maniac', things took an unexpected turn: 'Desmond sidled up to me in a room and said the song would be better if it had a couple more lines. Naively I said, 'Yes, what do you have in mind?' He said, 'Let's go in the other room', so Desmond, Alice and I batted around ideas and there were a couple of small lyrical changes'. Those changes amounted to the addition of the line, 'I'm crossing the line in my brain, the line between pleasure and pain'. That is it, nothing else about the song differs from the demo other than the banks of keyboards, the vocals and Chouinard's drum part.

The next development surprised Teeley: 'Within a day or two, Desmond said, 'You know we're gonna need some writer-ship on the song?' I said, 'I've got another writer on this; I don't know if he's gonna want to sign off on it, I don't know if I want to sign off on it'. Essentially Desmond said there's a lot of great songwriters, a lot of great songs out there and if you want your song on this record, then this is what it is'.

Held got a call from the publishing company saying that the credits were to be Desmond Child, Alice Cooper, Bob Held and Tom Teeley. He was furious: 'I said, that's not right. I get a call from Desmond saying if I don't play ball, he will take the song off the record. I said I was still not cool with this and he says to me, 'Bob, it's the music business; you gotta give and take'. I spoke to Don Glearson and he said, 'The record's mastered, nothing's coming off the record, so don't worry about anything'. I could have told Desmond to go screw himself, but he says to me: 'Bob, listen to me, I think you could be one of my inner circle guys'. I'm thinking that OK, I have to buy the ticket to get into the club. So we come up with the idea of a split on that song. I got 42%, Tom took 38%, and Desmond and Alice got 10% each. Desmond said to me, 'We have to have our names on the songs because the fans demand that'. I don't know how much Alice knew about what happened'.

Neither Held nor Teeley thinks the final version betters their demo. Held says: 'They recorded it in a lower key. I appreciate that the lyrics are very Alice-friendly and that's what did it. I am eternally thankful that the song was done by an iconic artist, but it's kind of lumpy; there's a lot more finesse and spring to the demo'. Teeley says that: 'I was never particularly thrilled with the song as it ended up because of that lack of high tension. But I was happy to have that song get picked up by a prominent artist. The lyrical weirdness lends to the impression (that Alice had more to do with writing it). My experience overall was a positive one. I had fun doing it. The run-in with the reality – to me, that was OK, that's the music business'.

'Trash' (Cooper/ Child/ Mark Frazier/ Jamie Sever)
The second great track is this balls-out rocker; another one that started life as a demo by outside writers, this time Mark Frazier and Jamie Sever from the band Unattached. Alice told *Metal Hammer* (July 1989) that: '(It) had a different title originally and was written by a band from Boston who played it to Desmond one day. We listened to the track later on, and liked it instantly. 'Trash' is an amazing rock 'n' roll song, musically as well as lyrically. I reworked the lyrics a little, Desmond looked through the arrangements and the song was ready!'

St. Jon agrees this is one of the best tracks: 'There are three or four strong songs on that record. I know that and the audience knows that too. It has a Rolling Stones feel'.

The decision to duet with Jon Bon Jovi was apparently down to Alice, who explained to *Circus* (1989) that: 'I wanted Jon to sing on 'Trash' because none of the stuff he ever sings is as nasty as that. I wanted him to sing on something that he wasn't allowed to sing on his album'. That was decent of Alice, but the song is not dramatically improved by his contribution. Alice would have handled it just fine alone, as evidenced when it was played live.

It's the first song with a largely different band. Aerosmith's rhythm section, Tom Hamilton and Joey Kramer play on it along with Mark Frazier and Jack Johnson. The big backing vocals are absent and there are few obvious keyboards either. The stripped-down style works well for this slick but dirty track. It has a life and rawness that excites from the opening riff and it never loses momentum. An excellent track that is lost in the sequencing.

'Hell Is Living Without You' (Cooper/ Child/ Jon Bon Jovi/ Richie Sambora)
It was recorded at Bearsville Studios and features stellar guest guitarists Steve Lukather and Richie Sambora.

McCurry says, 'Desmond loved Richie's playing and couldn't wait to get him on the record'. Sambora takes the solos on this inevitably Bon Jovi-esque track, which he co-wrote with Jon Bon Jovi and also features the then 'secret' member of that band on bass in the form of Hugh McDonald. Sadly the song drags and never really gets to any place of much interest. The chorus is dull, and a good Desmond Child song needs a strong chorus.

It opens with a synth and guitar intro, as per 'Poison'. Alice goes for a tortured, throaty vocal that plays off against those amazing backing vocals. The main problem is that there is little dynamic shift between the verses and the chorus, it all sounds a bit samey. The verses needed tightening up, while the chorus needed more power as the mid-tones are too soupy and indistinct. Sambora is the best thing about it, with a great solo that cuts through the mix. St. Jon worked hard on this one, explaining that: 'It's about giving the artist and producer the sounds they want to hear and the emotions you can blend into the song with your playing. Any kind of orchestration came from me'.

In the final analysis, the song misses the mark. It feels like more out of the 'Only My Heart Talkin'' box of average material. However, the backing vocals are excellent.

'I'm Your Gun' (Cooper/ Child/ McCurry)

McCurry's second writing credit came about because: 'I love Steve Stevens (from Billy Idol), he's a close friend of mine, so that's my bit of 'Rebel Yell' there, a fast version of it. Desmond didn't want anything to do with this song; he was like, 'What is this?' Alice and I did this whole thing, he was like, 'pull my trigger, I get bigger', just ridiculous. It was Spinal Tap meets Billy Idol. When Desmond and Alice came to me after I had done the lick for 'Poison', he said, 'Alice and I were talking. We feel that we should cut you in on the record', and Alice was behind him pointing at himself, so it was Alice who made sure I got my percentages'. So it was two credits for McCurry.

'I'm Your Gun' is the third great track, a high-energy closer with more of the pulse and crackle missing on much of the album. McCurry runs riot on guitar, while Alice turns in a barnstorming vocal with his best lyrics on the album. Kip Winger adds his distinctive vocal harmonies to great effect: 'That was the first time I met Desmond', he says. 'It was really great, I was in LA and they asked me to come down. I was at the height of my career, I had been in the band, so it made sense'.

The dramatic spoken introduction gives way to a headlong assault with McCurry, McDonald and Chouinard hammering out an adrenalin-filled rhythm that audibly seems to inspire Alice, who gleefully sings the tone-setting first verse: 'I'm dressed in black, I'm a heart attack, and my draw is lightning quick. If you're looking for a man with magic hands, I can really do the trick'. There's no let-up in the pace till the end of the track, with the only extra musical colour being some discrete keyboards. What a way to finish the album and what a shame we didn't get more songs like this!

Outtakes and related songs
'Aggrolat' (Cooper/Child/ McCurry)
This curiously named track baffles John McCurry, who has no
recollection of it all. It has been performed apparently by Chalmersspex
students at Chalmers University in Goteborg, Sweden. It has been
suggested to be an abbreviation for an aggressive latte!

'Ballad of Alice Cooper' (Cooper/ Child)
Registered at BMI as 'Alice Doesn't Live Here Anymore'. This one was
in the running for the album. Both Alice and Jon Bon Jovi (who would
have appeared on it) have spoken about it.

'Hold Back The Night' (Cooper/ Child)
Given to Robin Beck for her *Trouble Or Nothin'* album. This could easily
have fitted in on *Trash*. It has a Heart-like vibe to it and is a really good
song.

'Low Class Reunion' (Cooper/ Child)
One of the earliest songs written and would have been the title track
until the *Trash* concept took hold.

Other *Trash* era songs registered at BMI, but with no information, include:
'Bad Angel' (Cooper/ Child/ Diane Warren), **'Good Girl Gone Bad'**
(Cooper/ Child), **'Growin' Up The Hard Way'** (Cooper/ Child), **and**
'Sacred Heart' (Cooper/ Child)

Other appearances
Shocker (1989) (soundtrack album)
Alice appears on 'Shockdance', with a supergroup put together by Child
and called The Dudes Of Wrath. One dude was Guy Mann-Dude: 'It was
recorded at the Record Plant after the *Trash* sessions. 'Shockdance' was
kind of a throwaway tune that we wrote on the spot. I had some say in
the line-up. Desmond wanted a star-studded band, so I said to him, 'Get
Tommy Lee on drums and Rudy Sarzo on bass'. I think Desmond got
Vivian Campbell on guitar. I was surprised because it was like two days
later and Desmond got these guys! At the time, Desmond was so hot that
any musician would jump for joy to play for him! I was like, holy shit,
there's Tommy Lee! We all got along together with enthusiasm. Vivian

Campbell was great to work with. He was very musical and we were both there making music rather than battling each other. Tommy was excited about the next Motley Crue album and he played us a couple of cuts on his Walkman. Everybody was professional and played great'.

'Love Transfusion', also on the soundtrack and performed by Iggy Pop, was written by Alice, Desmond Child and Vladimir Matetski. This is a really good song that is better than several of the Cooper/ Child compositions on *Trash*.

Right Between The Eyes by Icon (Megaforce, 1989)

The album was produced by Icon's guitarist Dan Wexler, who went on to work with Alice on *The Last Temptation* and *Fistful Of Alice* albums. Alice performs a guest vocal on 'Two For The Road' and is the 'featured character voice' on 'Holy Man's War'. Neither track is essential but are well worth checking out if you want to dig deeper into Cooper world.

Trashes The World tour
31 October 1989 (Los Angeles, California) **to 27 October 1990** (Hollywood, California)

Setlist: 'Trash', 'Billion Dollar Babies', 'I'm Eighteen', 'I'm Your Gun', 'Desperado', 'No More Mr Nice Guy', 'This Maniac's In Love With You', 'Steven', 'Welcome To My Nightmare', 'The Ballad Of Dwight Fry', 'Gutter Cats Vs The Jets', 'Only Women Bleed', 'I Love The Dead', 'Poison', 'Muscle Of Love', 'Spark In The Dark', 'Is It My Body', 'House Of Fire', 'Bed Of Nails', 'School's Out', 'Under My Wheels'

Occasionally played: 'Is It My Body', 'Cold Ethyl', 'The Awakening', 'Department Of Youth', 'He's Back (The Man Behind The Mask)', 'Only My Heart Talkin''

Al Pitrelli's guitar solo came before 'Poison', and the drum solo came before 'Bed Of Nails'

Musicians: Al Pitrelli (lead guitar), Pete Friesen (guitar), Derek Sherinian (keyboards), Tommy 'T-Bone' Caradonna (bass), Jonathan Mover & Eric Singer (drums), Devon Meade (vocals, performer).

(Jonathan Mover left after 22 January 1990, and was replaced by Eric Singer for all subsequent dates)

Initial thoughts were to use four of the core band from the *Trash* album for the backing musicians. But, as Alice explained to Guitar (February 1990), 'the band just wasn't available for the tour'. In the case of Chouinard and St. Jon, their immediate loyalties were to their regular employer. St. Jon confirms that 'They asked me to do the tour, but I couldn't because I had to go back out with Squier. They also asked Bobby to do the tour, but he was also rejoining Squier. We had been with him since '78, so we had to stay loyal'. Hugh McDonald was equally tied up with Bon Jovi, which just left John McCurry.

Alice and McCurry had grown close over the making of *Trash,* so he felt this was his new live lead guitarist and band leader. But McCurry felt unable to do it: 'Alice asked me to go on tour with him, right after they did the video for 'Poison'. I had been out on tour nearly non-stop since 1983, I was never home and I needed a break. But Shep Gordon reached out to my lawyer in New York saying, 'Alice would like John to go on tour'. My lawyer called me in and I said, 'I don't want to go on tour; just kindly decline the offer. Just say I need a mental and physical break from touring, but I hope we can continue to be friends. Let me call Alice'. My lawyer said, 'Absolutely not – you don't have any dealings with him; I will deal with Shep. We have to ask for a sum of money; what's a crazy number?' McCurry pulled $5,000 a week out of the air, not really thinking anything of it, especially when his lawyer got a 'negative reaction' from Shep to the figure. The offer was over, it seemed, but no. 'About a day later, Shep called my lawyer back and said Alice had agreed to $5,000 a week'. Despite his lawyer's enthusiasm, McCurry still did not change his mind. 'That is the last time I had any dealings with Alice or Shep', he says. 'It doesn't mean Alice wouldn't speak with me now, but to say his feelings were hurt is probably an understatement'.

So video-taped auditions were duly set up at Leeds Rehearsals in Los Angeles to recruit a band. Alice turned to a former hired gun for help in selecting the band – Arti Funaro. Funaro recalls the process: 'Alice and I picked each player. He assessed the look of them, but also expressed his like or dislike of their playing. We had a code. I can't tell you what it is since he may still be using it. I recommended only the very best players musically, and Alice had the final say on their image, etc. I heard later that although they were amazing players, they acted like divas and were very expensive. So Alice went another route with the whole thing and started over. I don't blame him. But man, could they play! There were about 100 or so that didn't make the cut. Some known within the industry, most others unknown'.

Pete Friesen was selected for the special quality he brought to the sound. Alice told *Guitar* (February 1990), 'I picked Pete because he's so solid, so nailed to the ground. He's a young kid, but he knows all the original material, the 'No More Mr. Nice Guy' stuff, so he refuses to budge. He plays it like the record and will not move. I think that's great. He's dedicated to recreating music, a real '70s head. I think that's unique for a kid of 23'. That was a significant turnaround by Alice from the attitude on the two previous tours.

Tommy 'T-Bone' Caradonna had toured with Lita Ford but now found himself looking for work, 'back in Hollywood on the couch and floor tour' as he puts it. The break came when he was tipped off that Alice was going to be auditioning. 'I was put in contact with Brian Nelson, who was awesome. The songs we auditioned were classic Alice songs, 'No More Mr. Nice Guy', 'School's Out', 'Under My Wheels' etc. It was a cattle call. Everybody and their mother was auditioning. I got to play with Carlos Cavazo and Frankie Banali. They were cool. I got called back seven times during the process while auditioning the other players. The first hired were Pete on guitar who appeared playing bass in the 'Poison' video, myself, and a drummer named Eddie Steele. Eddie's brother was Steve, who played bass for Alice on a previous tour'.

With Caradonna, Friesen and Eddie Steele in place, they still needed a lead guitarist/band leader plus a keyboard player.

Next in was Al Pitrelli, who says 'Steve Vai was a great friend and always very supportive of me. Around middle/late September, I got a call. Alice Cooper wanted to speak to me. Steve was their first choice, but he was committed to Whitesnake. He said to them, 'Al Pitrelli would be your guy and musical director'. September 26 – I remember exactly because it was my birthday; Alice's people called up from LA and that was the beginning of an incredible journey'.

Pitrelli came in and made an instant impression, says Caradonna. 'There were some songs on the new record that were VSO'd (varispeeded), so the key was shifted was up a half step or so. A lot of people figured it out in the wrong key. But when it came to playing it, Al moved it up a half step and said OK, ready to go. He transposed everything in his head, solos everything. That was very impressive! By the grace of God, I figured it out when I was learning the material'.

Pitrelli knew who they should get on keyboards: 'I went to college with Derek Sherinian. When Alice was saying, 'You got anybody in mind for keyboards?' I said, 'Yeah, I know this guy who is awesome'. So Alice says let's get him in. I called Derek up and I said, 'Listen, I recommended you to come in, but I am just gonna tell you one thing,

'Come in and play, do not speak', because I knew how Derek could be. We both laughed at that, but he came in as Derek Sherinian does, well-prepared and Alice was like, 'Cool'.

Things were still not right with the 'final' line-up. Caradonna explains that: 'We were now having trouble with the drummer. Al wasn't confident with Eddie Steele, so we went through a lot of drummers. Alice wanted to put a trap door under the drum kit – his awesome sense of humour! They finally decided on Jonathan Mover, who just did great, totally prepared and pro. It didn't hurt that he was on the cover of *Modern Drummer* that month'. In fact, it was Pitrelli who suggested Mover after the others had failed to impress. 'I knew we needed somebody special', he says.

Jonathan Mover recalls that: 'I got back from Moscow in mid-September to a bunch of frantic phone messages from Alive Entertainment: 'Please call us immediately, we desperately need a drummer and you've been recommended by several people. I knew a lot of Alice's early catalogue, *Welcome To My Nightmare* being my favourite, so I was ready to play. Obviously, they wanted me to learn the *Trash* album. I don't recall how I got a copy, maybe it was already released and I picked it up, or they overnighted it to me. I listened to it the next morning on the flight to LA for Alice. To be clear on this, I wasn't asked to come out to audition; I was asked to come and do the gig. I got to the rehearsal studio, met the guys, and we began playing 'Trash'. We did a verse and a chorus and then Alice stopped the band, turned around to me and said, 'Welcome to the band, go talk to 'so and so' to go over the details'. Now, before I even got on the plane to LA, I told them how much my weekly fee was and they agreed. As soon as I got there, played and solidified the gig, I sat down with 'so and so' and he offered me well below my fee and what they had already agreed to. I politely said, 'Thank you very much for the offer and opportunity. I've got a couple of students that I can recommend'. I won't tell you what his reply was, but upon hearing it, I stood up, turned around and began walking out the door. He begrudgingly came back at me, agreeing to my fee, but asked me to keep it a secret from all the others, who would be making much less'.

Apart from Eddie Steele, Carlos Cavazo and Frankie Banali (both Quiet Riot), other musicians who didn't make the cut were drummer Curly Smith (later with Boston), Mark St. John (briefly lead guitarist in Kiss) and Tracii Guns (L.A. Guns). Caradonna remembers Tracii because he, 'Was trying to convince me to get a vampire bite tattoo on my neck. Also, guys from the band Autograph auditioned'.

To go some way to reproduce the *Trash* album backing vocals, it was decided to bring in one more recruit. Devon Meade recalls: 'My boyfriend at the time was Curly Smith. He auditioned as the drummer and he said they needed a singer. I got the gig, but he didn't. That didn't go well for our relationship. It was Desmond who hired me. Because he produced it with stacked backing vocals, they had to have someone like me'. Devon says that the first step was to record new backing vocals in Child's studio. She was asked to go there and lay down the tracks. These tracks were then rendered as patches which were probably triggered by Sherinian. 'This was right before the whole pre-recorded concert vocals, Janet Jackson drama,' she points out. 'I sang the high parts live, and the guys would gang up too'.

But as well as being a visible backing vocalist, they were also interested in Meade's performance skills. 'As well as a singer, I was a trained dancer, so they asked me if I would dye my hair black and was I willing to have my throat cut! Are you willing to be on stage to be a featured performer? I said, 'Yes sure', so I was the maniacal nurse and I got strangled in 'Only Women Bleed' and also had my throat cut during the show. I was very busy. I was onstage or offstage costume changing, or I was singing. I sang on most of the songs, backing vocals/gang vocals. The vocals weren't all that challenging, but I loved the work onstage; it was fun'. The stage crew filled out the other performance parts needed. Caradonna's tech Batty was one of the street gang who take on Alice, for example.

The time spent preparing the show had been longer than normal for Alice, but he was determined to get it right, with some input from Epic. He told *Hit Parader* (1990) that: 'They're trying to get me back on top again, and they're doing a great job. They haven't really talked to me about it, but I know they'd prefer if the show didn't totally turn off the executives of the label. There's still blood this time, but I've placed the focus on other areas. The show is still pretty wild, but the focus this time will be just as much on the music as it is on the visuals'.

Pitrelli started his musical director role at rehearsals: 'I took it seriously because it was such a huge tour and such a big record for him. I worked really hard, scrutinising everything to bring it to life. The thing with Alice's music is really that there's a lot to it. You had to dig in deep to learn it'.

The setlist was effectively a refresher on Alice Cooper's past, combined with a current best-selling album for new fans. Only 'He's Back' put in an appearance from the 'metal' albums, and that was only once! Pitrelli says that the selections were, 'Mostly down to Alice and Shep. They had a pretty clear idea of what songs they wanted to bring back and present. I mean, he had such huge success with 'Poison' and the *Trash* album; he was bang on top of the world. I was a big fan of the original band when they brought out songs like 'Under My Wheels' and 'Muscle Of Love'. To stand next to that man and play 'Eighteen' and all those incredible songs I grew up listening to – that was the time of my life'. The deep surprise inclusion, and Pitrelli delight, was the never played live before 'Desperado'.

The set was going to be a long one too. Alice told *Kerrang* (December 1989) that: 'We are doing 26 songs: almost the entire *Trash* album and classics like 'Muscle Of Love', 'Gutter Cats Vs The Jets', 'Desperado', 'Cold Ethyl' and 'The Ballad Of Dwight Fry'. It's an hour-and-45-minute show. I'm not doing theatre in every song. There's a goodly amount, but I'd rather do more songs because, again, it's something different. We'll rock 'n' roll a little more. We've got more material with as much theatre, only it's a longer show, with a few new wrinkles, and that's what's taking so long'.

One of the wrinkles was 'Steven', which would see Alice going backstage to have his eye makeup applied, shown on film to the audience. The song, as they rehearsed it, wasn't long enough and they needed something for a suitable crescendo as Alice returned to the stage. Pitrelli came up with the solution: 'They needed 30 or 40 seconds extra music that didn't exist to go along with the film they had. I remember coming up with something on the fly that was pretty cool. That was Alice saying, 'What have you got?' I was able to look at the film and say; I think something like this would be appropriate. He said, 'Oh, I like that very much'. That was a great day for me!'

The set was organised into three sections. The first section featured the band rocking out on a mix of Cooper classics and oldies; a seven-song punch with 'Desperado' offering the only real diversity. The opening one-two attack saw them deliver a harder-hitting 'Trash' followed by the first oldie of the set, 'Billion Dollar Babies'. Mover says, 'Each drummer I've heard play it does it in his own way. I'm not sure if that's because they're struggling to play what Neal (Smith) played, or they're just putting their own spin on it and playing it their own way. As for me, I love what Neal played, which is very creative and certainly not what the average drummer of the time would have played. That being said, I played it with my own twist, which was to incorporate (thirty-second-note) double-bass figures in between the main snare phrases, as well as in the main groove'.

There were still the obvious differences between the older material and the *Trash* songs. Mover found the earlier songs more enjoyable to play: 'Alice's material isn't very hard to play; you just have to be able to navigate through all the arrangements. Songs like 'Billion Dollar Babies', 'Welcome To My Nightmare', 'Under My Wheels' and 'Muscle Of Love' were certainly more fun to play than, say, 'Poison' or 'House Of Fire'. But that doesn't mean I didn't like to play the newer material; it just means that I enjoyed playing the older material more for compositional as well as nostalgic reasons. It's always a thrill when you get to play a song that you grew up listening to, with the actual artist that wrote and recorded it'.

'The Awakening' was in the set from the off but was soon dropped to improve the pacing of the middle of the show. One or two other songs appeared in the set. Caradonna: 'They added certain songs in certain markets like 'Department Of Youth' in Australia and I remember doing 'Man Behind The Mask' somewhere in Europe'.

Part two, beginning with 'Steven', saw Alice beset by his nightmares again. For half an hour, the theatrics were a big part of the show, commencing with the straitjacket routine, moving through a gangland ruck on 'Gutter Cat' where Caradonna got to play the cool bass intro. 'It was wonderful learning Dennis's bass lines; he was great, and always came up with such brilliant ideas. That intro to 'Gutter Cat' was a bit of pieced-together harmonic bass that I had dicked around with prior to Alice and adapted it to the song's intro. Then Alice lighting my cigarette was pretty fucking cool too. That was his idea, I can't take credit for that'. That intro led straight into a brief riff on 'Singing In The Rain', which Caradonna says, 'Was a nod to *Clockwork Orange*. Again Alice's awesome sense of humour'. Meade adds 'The roadies were the Jets. I played every single person that got killed in the show; I just wore a different costume!' After the gangland death scene, it culminated with the guillotine and 'I Love The Dead'.

The final third was a return to the arena rock jukebox hits of part one, commencing with 'Poison' which featured Pitrelli's solo before it. He says that 'Alice was all about guitar hero stuff back then and he just wanted to have that moment before 'Poison' so I wanted to do something special. Everyone seemed to enjoy it, so it allowed me to dig into my Gary Moore world a little bit. It became such a spot in the show, but again, it went to my head. I took it too far, but that was a really nice spot. It was musical and it flowed into 'Poison' quite well. I remember squatting or bending my knees in these incredible arenas and stadiums, looking up, thinking this is my dream come true'. The encore was 'party time' as always with 'School's Out', but more excitingly finished with the high-octane 'Under My Wheels'.

The first show was at the Cathouse in Los Angeles on 31 October. This back-to-roots gig was perfect for blowing off the cobwebs before heading to Europe for the opening dates of *Trashes The World*. The first 'proper' date was in Brussels (Forest National, 21 November). It was particularly memorable for Caradonna: 'My tech Batty wasn't there for pre-productions in LA but was going to join us in Brussels. I had never met him prior to that, and I don't know if they knew for sure what tech position he was going to be doing. So we're going to the stage for the first show, lights go down and the audience starts roaring. It's black, so the tech that was doing me and Pete handed me my Fender 69 P bass with only three strings on it. He said the G string kept breaking when he put it on, so he decided that three strings were enough! The stage manager is flashing his light, signalling Coop's ready and in place, and we're ready with the intro of 'Hello Hooray'. Needless to say, the Italian that I am, I about had a nuclear brain vomit. Here I am with every judgemental cunt waiting for me to fuck up! Right then, Kenny Barr (who was Al's tech), and Batty came over to string up my bass. Disaster avoided. They are angels and the best techs, so I'm forever grateful'.

Caradonna, like Pete Friesen, felt a reverence for the old songs. 'I loved playing all the classic Alice songs from the original band with Dennis on it, and also the *Welcome to My Nightmare* material with Prakash John, who is another great bass player'.

The band were outstandingly impressive, playing the old songs with bite and reverence but giving the *Trash* songs a raw, exciting edge that had been smoothed over in the album's production. Caradonna appreciates the praise for the band. 'We just played it full of piss and vinegar', he says. Alice was more eloquent when he enthused to *Raw* (1989) that, 'This is such a great rock 'n' roll band, such a bunch of great street rats!'

Pitrelli agrees: 'That was one of the things that I was so grateful to Alice for. He said, 'Bring it to life; let's see what you got'. He was really interested in seeing what we could do to them live. They weren't replicated exactly because he gave me carte blanche to put a bit extra on the songs. I heard from a lot of people like it was really going back to the original band. I give a lot of credit to Pete Friesen and T-Bone. That '70s sound was their bag; then you had Derek Sherinian, Jonathan

Mover and I who were from a different school. The combination of those elements came together well. That was a very special chemistry that band had'.

Mover has a very different view on the band chemistry: 'Any artist hiring a band would love there to be chemistry, camaraderie and a vibe. In most of my career opportunities, that's not really a factor because although I've been associated with some artists long-term, I'm basically a freelance player and always going from one to another. My job is to make sure the artist is happy. If there are differences within the band, that becomes secondary and you just deal with it, focusing on pleasing the artist that hired you. But, with this situation in particular, the band didn't really gel very well, which was a combination of personalities, professional experience, and musical abilities, or lack thereof, for some. Two guys in the band were excellent players that came from serious music school studies, and two guys were more street players. I was trying to find the middle ground in between, which wasn't always so easy. So I don't think the band was as good as it could have been. Mind you, there were some nights that we were on fire, but that was usually when three of us played a little more simply, and even so, it wasn't consistent from night to night'.

Devon Meade enjoyed the shows: 'They ran like clockwork. We got into a groove with the routines, the costume changes, 'OK, you wear this and you go there'. The whole show was choreographed. All the backgrounds were me, so the guys just lip-synched. Watch the Birmingham film – the vocals still continue when they step away from their mics'. Pitrelli holds his hands up and agrees: 'Yeah, well none of us could really sing, so we needed some help. I mean, we could all sing OK and gang up on 'School's Out'. But you're talking about songs like 'Poison' or 'House Of Fire'. The big production songs off that record had a lot of vocals going on and Devon did a great job singing'. Mover observes that: 'She was a real trooper and a total professional. I know of very few people who would have put up with all that she did on a daily basis and still deliver a top-notch performance every night, musically, physically and emotionally'. Meade, for her part, says that 'Al was an amazing player and Jonathan Mover was an incredible drummer, so was Eric Singer. They were the cream of the crop'. But offstage, there were issues, which Mover alluded to, that would dog the tour.

Pitrelli was finding it hard to adjust as he dealt with personal issues: 'It was everything I ever dreamed of, to travel the world and play all these venues. I mean, one of the first shows we did was playing Wembley. I was like, this kind of works, you know? In my case, I had dreamt about it since I saw The Beatles on *Ed Sullivan*. In the beginning with Alice, it was like a dream come true, but if you have issues to deal with, going on that kind of touring, is like pouring gasoline on a fire. Immaturity got the best of me. I insulted enough people to the point where they said, 'Fuck this kid!'

To the audiences, what struck everyone was just how great Pitrelli was, a real rock star lead guitarist with huge talent. Pitrelli reveals, 'There's a little bit of a facade that goes on with that. Insecurity will get the best of you, you know? That was always part of the issue. You are trying to suppress a lot of insecurity. But when you get that opportunity, you are like, 'I'm gonna show everybody'. I always felt at home with a guitar around my neck and I loved being part of a great ensemble. Alice was good at giving us confidence: 'You all deserve to be here; you guys are awesome so go enjoy'. What you don't realise when you're young is it really doesn't have that much to do with your musicality or your abilities as a musician. It's mostly got to do with whether you a good human being who can get on with people and not be a fucking asshole. I was guilty of being a fucking asshole. I had a lot of growing up to do'.

Meade's issues started quickly. She singles out the night of the Marquee Club performance in England as the beginning: 'I was green, still very young. We did our first show In England, and in front of everybody (one of the tour party) said, 'You're a really cool chick, but you're gonna be even cooler when I fuck you'. That was the beginning. Some of those guys were horrible. They were morons. I was tormented on the tour. I was like, no one's going to get me to quit, so I stayed and the horrible behaviour continued'.

Mover sees it like this: 'The problem was that everyone in the band, with exception to me (and Alice), had an extreme dislike of the female singer/actor, Devon. I'm sure everyone had their own reason(s), but we got on fine. She was an excellent singer, theatrically played the various roles very well, and was very easy to get along with, not to mention look at. *She* was not the problem. I felt terribly that she was the pin-cushion of the tour, but boys will be boys, and I wasn't around long enough to witness the really nasty stuff go down, though I heard about it later on'.

Meade was alone in a 'boys night out' world: 'I had a dressing room next to theirs. They got into town, getting strippers and chicks. In order for me to get to my wardrobe, I had to walk through naked women, strippers and all stages of anything. That was pretty much two or three shows a week. I went into observation mode. If I was on the bus, I would be reading, or listening to music or sleeping. Inside I was screaming. Alice was the absolute best to me. He was my protector. Alice looked out for me over and over again, mainly because the band was so crazy, and everything that goes along with that. You're a backing singer in that kind of situation, so you're either a bitch or a slut. I did not do anything, so I became the bitch'.

She eventually sought help from one of the management: 'The tour was misogynistic'. One time one of the guys was really bad. We were in Canada and he was knocking on my door. I went and said to management, 'This is abusive and I don't know what to do'. He looked at me and said, 'You don't know what abuse is, Devon, until he hits you over the head. Then you can come back to me'. I just never complained anymore, but Alice knew'. One strategic move coming from Alice was to keep her close by him when possible. Meade is still grateful: 'Alice was wonderful; I had no problems with the performance. I got to go to the soundcheck with Alice. He protected me when he could. I have nothing but 100% pure admiration for Alice. He never treated me with anything but respect and kindness'.

Musically there were sticking points that arose too. Mover points out that: 'Due to the musical, rhythmic and educational influences in my life, my vocabulary is anything but straight 4/4 and/or average. Since it's my vocabulary, it doesn't seem 'out' or difficult to me. Because of that, I was naturally throwing in things like quintuplets, broken tuplets, fills over the bar line, displacing accents, playing with the time; things that are simple to me but can be quite foreign and confusing to others that aren't used to hearing them or counting them. I believe it was in 'I Love The Dead', where I had a few solo drum fills to play, so I would often throw in something not-so-ordinary and inevitably lose one or two guys along the way. Pitrelli came up to me one night and gave me an earful about playing a fill that consisted of quintuplets or fives. My immediate reaction was to tell him to go teach the others how to count, which of course, wasn't very professional of me, but there was already a lot of headbutts within the band and so I wasn't cutting them much slack. Anyway, my literal reply was, 'Those were perfectly executed fives', which of course, made Pitrelli crack up, as did I, which solidified our friendship and mutual musical respect for each other even more. Needless to say, I did start to dumb it down from that point on. 'Perfectly Executed Fives' became a catchphrase for the rest of the tour'.

The drum solo was another sticking point for Mover: 'I would prefer to 'play' within the songs, rather than on my own, but Alice wanted a big rock drum solo, and I had certainly played them in the past. So, I did the kind of solo that I used to do with Satriani and/or any of the 'muso' gigs I had done previously. Even though I was playing what I thought was some cool shit, I don't recall anything special with regard to audience reaction. About a week into the tour, Alice pulled me aside and told me I was playing over the audience's heads: 'Instead of doing all that technical mumbo jumbo, do something like slow down, speed up, and do some fast double bass with a lot of crashes' etc. The next drum solo went down like a storm!'

The success of the album and singles was being matched by sell-out shows in big venues. Europe was followed by a month of Canadian dates, beginning on 28 December in Ottawa. The leg actually finished with a performance on 22 January 1990 at the American Music Awards at the Shrine Civic Auditorium in Hollywood. They performed 'House Of Fire', and it was an ending of sorts with Jonathan Mover playing his last gig of the tour. He left because of, 'Money, plain and simple, for good and bad reasons. The bad reason was that my checks began bouncing. I won't get into the hows and whys, although I did find out later on that it was not at all directly related to Shep or Alice. At the same time that their debt to me was building up, Joe Satriani was calling and graciously offering a nice raise to win me back. My last two weeks with Alice had me flying back and forth to San Francisco on every day off to rehearse with Joe and then back to Canada the next day to play with Alice. It was exhilarating and exhausting, but I was living the dream. After the awards show, I went straight from the stage to the airport, flew to Vancouver and was onstage with Joe later that same night and for the rest of '90'.

Time was now spent working in new drummer Eric Singer before the first American tour. The first leg ran from 23 February, with the new single 'Only My Heart Talkin'' added to the setlist after 'Spark In The Dark'.

The drummer switch made quite a difference due to Singer having a very different style from Mover. Pitrelli says, 'Both were great drummers. Jonathan had his way of articulating his musicality and Eric had a different way. I was a huge fan of Jonathan's, but Eric was awesome as well. By the time Eric got into the band, I was going through a lot of problems, a whole bunch of turmoil back home in New York'.

Alice, speaking to *Metal Hammer* (May 1990), looked to the positives while also, unfortunately, downplaying Mover's contributions: 'The drum sound is great now; it's just as heavy as we wanted it to be from the start. I think Eric fits in with this band better, at least musically. He plays the songs just like I like them to be played with a strong bass drum, so it's very heavy and very straight. Jonathan was more of a playful drummer who knew loads of tricks; he was a great technician but not as hard and heavy when it came to banging the skins, which just happens to be best for Alice Cooper'.

The man who was best placed to judge the switch was Caradonna: 'Both Jonathan and Eric are great drummers. But yes, both had different playing styles. You get used to and comfortable with one player, then they're gone, so you just have to adapt to the new one. There wasn't much time for auditions and they only had a handful of applicants, all of whom were great drummers'.

With little break, the next leg was a trip to Australia and New Zealand, followed by a return to Europe. In Europe, Meade remembers one of Alice's cardinal rules getting broken: 'In the beginning of the tour Alice made it clear there were to be no drugs on the bus. We were going into Hungary from Yugoslavia and they started laughing once we got through the border. Alice said, 'What?', and they replied, 'Ooh, we got the hash through'. Oh my God, Al nearly got fired. From then on, Alice and his entourage went across borders in a car while the other guys went on the bus'.

After Europe came Alice's first-ever dates in Japan. It was there that things finally boiled over between Meade and Pitrelli. It was supposed to be a prank, but Meade saw it differently: 'We were in NKH Hall, Tokyo. I did a duet with Alice called 'Only My Heart Talkin'' where I would sing my ass off. Al and T-Bone cross-patched my floor monitor with T-Bone's. Al Pitrelli was laughing his ass off because he set it up, so T-Bone was singing in my monitor while I was singing a duet with Alice. Alice was just looking at me and they thought it was the funniest thing ever. I just saw red. I walked off stage while we were waiting for the encores. I took all my rings off my left hand and put them on my right hand, thinking, 'This will hurt him'. Al walked off stage and I cold caught him in the face. When I punched him, he punched me back, but I am tiny, so he sent me flying. Alice walks off stage and he calls to a bodyguard, 'Get Devon,' so he picks me up. Al starts walking towards me again, so I picked up one of his guitars, soaking it in water and ruined it. He went for the guitar rather than going for me. The bodyguard got me to the dressing room and I thought, 'Oh my God, I am so fired'. There was a knock on the door. I said, 'Come in' and it was Alice. He looked at me, but he started laughing and he said, 'What took you so long?' I laughed too. It was just what it took; I had toughened up. They never messed with me again. Al Pitrelli went to management, wanting me to pay for his guitar. They said, 'No, you got yourself into it; you get yourself out of it'.

A few more dates followed, concluding in October 1990 in Los Angeles and Arizona, but then that was it, the end of *Trashes The World*.

Friesen, Sherinian and Singer would be back for the *Hey Stoopid* tour, but the others left. Pitrelli was dismissed but has an open and honest take on what happened: 'We took great pride in creating a great band. Alice was a great leader and a great boss. I know that I was putting myself in not the best light at that time with Alice and his camp. On a personal level, I was doing some goofy shit. I was young and I was going through a lot of issues, but I was no longer like the little prince if you will. I started letting things get to my head. I was 27 years old and I would rage and carry on like an asshole. I did a couple of interviews where I said some stupid things 'coz I wasn't thinking. I pissed off enough people where they said, 'No, we can't have that, fuck off'. That was devastating at the time, to say the least, but in retrospect, it was one of the best things that ever happened to me. I ran into Alice some years ago and he and a bunch of his band came to our show (Trans-Siberian Orchestra). After the show, he looked at me with that big old smile of his saying, 'Aren't you glad I fired you?!' And I said, 'Yes sir!' So at the end of the day, it all worked out pretty well. It was an important life lesson, a big blow, but I deserved dismissal. My personality wasn't working out the way they had wanted it'.

Caradonna says he just 'Wasn't asked back for the next tour', but no reasons were given. As for Devon Meade, she is philosophical about the tour: 'It was a different world back then and I am not saying it was OK. But here's the thing, it didn't ruin my experience at all. I had a ball. I'm the only woman who has ever sung on stage with Alice. I do tell people I was extremely lucky. How many women got, or get, to experience a true rock 'n' roll tour as I did?'

National Exhibition Centre, Birmingham, 13 and 14 December 1989 (DVD)

The film is a superb multi-camera shot record of the show featuring the band and Alice on excellent form. It is astoundingly good, in fact, given how early it was in the tour. Pitrelli still marvels at the recording: 'When

I go back to listen to the live show from Birmingham, it is still awesome, and that was pretty much a live take – great energy, great vibe'.

It was a show that Mover will never forget: 'The weather in Europe, and Scandinavia in particular, was freezing and it was snowing quite a bit. I ended up with pneumonia and found myself in hospital in Helsinki. Due to some very serious non-stop coughing before I got on antibiotics, I ended up with two hairline-fractured ribs. Breathing wasn't too bad, but playing had become pretty painful. They shot me up with some meds and gave me more to take with me. They also put a tight velcro wrap around my waist and chest to prohibit me from moving too much onstage and in general. I wore it under my t-shirt from that night on, but no one knew until it was time to film the show in Birmingham. Someone from the film crew asked me to play shirtless. I obliged, and for the first of the two shows there, which was the one being filmed and recorded, I took the wrap off and went for it. It was a painful show, but it was one of the best performances of the entire tour, so it was worth it. The band was pumped to nail it, and absolutely did. We all left the arena with a sense of accomplishment. We then came into soundcheck the next day for the second show and found out that the audio from the previous night was corrupted, so we had to do it all over again. Needless to say, we were all pretty deflated. We repeated the show, but it wasn't nearly as good, and we all knew it. On top of that, because I had to play without the wrap for another night to match the video footage, the pain was ten times worse. So, the live *Trash* concert video was the second show, which seriously paled in comparison to the night before'.

While the audio is from the second night, It seems likely that footage was used from both nights and synced where necessary. Epic made use of the soundtrack to bolster their compilation *Classicks* (1995). Alongside their debatable choices from the studio works they owned, they also picked the following from Birmingham: 'Under My Wheels', 'Billion Dollar Babies', 'I'm Eighteen', 'No More Mr. Nice Guy', 'Only Women Bleed' and 'School's Out'.

The album that never happened

Metal Hammer (May 1990) reported that Alice, the *Trashes the World* touring band, and Desmond Child would be taking a working break in Hawaii. Alice said, 'We'll start writing the first songs and developing ideas. At the moment, I'm thinking of developing very basic ideas and structures, but I'll return to the States with the band to continue developing ideas in a place where rock 'n' roll is created best. The most authentic surroundings are very simply a garage!' *Kerrang* (April 1990) also picked up on this, reporting that Spike and Guy from Quireboys were to submit material, including a song called 'I Like It', which they had originally offered too late for *Trash*.

Alice and Child already had songs; the *Trash* leftovers plus new ones, including the still unrecorded 'Your Love Is My Prison'. Equally, Caradonna and Sherinian had come up with two songs – 'If Fourth Street Could Talk' and 'Drowning In The Jealous Sea'. Both were offered to Alice, who liked them enough to get the returning Dick Wagner to add something to them.

Meanwhile, Alice was also writing songs alone with Wagner and seven still exist in demo form: 'As Long As My Heart Holds Out', 'I'm Gonna Haunt Your House', 'Keeping My Eye On The Time', 'Message In Your Madness', 'Misery Train', 'Thief Of Hearts' and 'You Fed Me To The Wolves'.

Another song called 'Hard Baby To Rock' also exists, written by Cooper, Wagner, Georgia Leigh Middleman and Vivian Ray.

'Chemical Reaction', also written by Wagner and Alice, plus Pete Dantillo, is the only one to come out in the public domain, emerging in great quality on YouTube. Susan Michelson observes that: 'Most of those Dick wrote to start with and then brought Alice in. That's often how they worked in the later years'. All of the Cooper/Wagner songs listed above are excellent and would have worked well on *Hey Stoopid*. 'Hard Baby To Rock' with an Eddie Cochran groove and killer chorus is a huge loss in particular.

The American dates due in May/June 1990 were cancelled to make time for the band to look at the songs. Pitrelli confirms: 'During a break in the tour, we went to a studio in LA and we were doing demos. Desmond Child was producing it, Arthur Payson was the engineer. Dick Wagner came in because he had written some songs. It was really exciting. With an opportunity like that and with a record on the horizon, we all wanted to be in the band. Alice was so gracious and said, 'You guys got any material?' It was incredible'.

Unfortunately, says Pitrelli, 'I was ridiculously annoying. The only thing I saw was me, I want more; I need this, I need that. I was like, 'Hey, listen to this demo; I got this idea', and I got back, 'Hey kid, just shut up!' With time now running out for Pitrelli, spending time with Wagner was a great memory: 'Dick Wagner, what a great guy. You could sit down and talk to him. What he had achieved in his career as a guitar player and songwriter was incredible. It was an honour and a privilege to be there. One of the songs I fell in love with that we were working on was 'Might As Well Be On Mars'. What a great piece of music. I wanted to pick his brain, but instead of being patient, I was just like this annoying little kid. But he was a gentleman and a pleasure to work with'.

Another song that was eventually picked up for *Hey Stoopid* was 'Burning Our Bed', which started off as a Pitrelli song. 'It was a good song', he sighs, 'and it really stung that I didn't get to play on it for the album'.

Other than demos, no actual recording sessions took place by the touring band and all we have left are the quality demos which Dick Wagner recorded with Alice. They deserve to be widely heard.

Epilogue: Following on from Trash

After pulling the plug on the touring band, Alice went for safer ground and followed up *Trash* with *Hey Stoopid* (1991), which didn't hit the same mark in terms of sales but was arguably a more satisfying record. He followed that with the superb *The Last Temptation* in 1994, an album that is right up there with his best work. From there, things stuttered with record company problems. He remained a big draw on stage throughout the nineties, as evidenced by the live album *A Fistful Of Alice* (1997), but apart from one studio song, there was nothing else new. Alice needed a change of focus and direction, so fortunately, as the decade drew to a close, he came up with it. *Brutal Planet* (2000) was shocking, vibrant and unmistakably Alice. It was the catalyst for over twenty years now of sustained quality albums and hugely successful tours, not to mention the best reunion we could have hoped for.

On Track series

Alan Parsons Project – Steve Swift 978-1-78952-154-2

Tori Amos – Lisa Torem 978-1-78952-142-9

Asia – Peter Braidis 978-1-78952-099-6

Badfinger – Robert Day-Webb 978-1-878952-176-4

Barclay James Harvest – Keith and Monica Domone 978-1-78952-067-5

The Beatles – Andrew Wild 978-1-78952-009-5

The Beatles Solo 1969-1980 – Andrew Wild 978-1-78952-030-9

Blue Oyster Cult – Jacob Holm-Lupo 978-1-78952-007-1

Blur – Matt Bishop – 978-178952-164-1

Marc Bolan and T.Rex – Peter Gallagher 978-1-78952-124-5

Kate Bush – Bill Thomas 978-1-78952-097-2

Camel – Hamish Kuzminski 978-1-78952-040-8

Caravan – Andy Boot 978-1-78952-127-6

Cardiacs – Eric Benac 978-1-78952-131-3

Eric Clapton Solo – Andrew Wild 978-1-78952-141-2

The Clash – Nick Assirati 978-1-78952-077-4

Crosby, Stills and Nash – Andrew Wild 978-1-78952-039-2

The Damned – Morgan Brown 978-1-78952-136-8

Deep Purple and Rainbow 1968-79 – Steve Pilkington 978-1-78952-002-6

Dire Straits – Andrew Wild 978-1-78952-044-6

The Doors – Tony Thompson 978-1-78952-137-5

Dream Theater – Jordan Blum 978-1-78952-050-7

Electric Light Orchestra – Barry Delve 978-1-78952-152-8

Elvis Costello and The Attractions – Georg Purvis 978-1-78952-129-0

Emerson Lake and Palmer – Mike Goode 978-1-78952-000-2

Fairport Convention – Kevan Furbank 978-1-78952-051-4

Peter Gabriel – Graeme Scarfe 978-1-78952-138-2

Genesis – Stuart MacFarlane 978-1-78952-005-7

Gentle Giant – Gary Steel 978-1-78952-058-3

Gong – Kevan Furbank 978-1-78952-082-8

Hall and Oates – Ian Abrahams 978-1-78952-167-2

Hawkwind – Duncan Harris 978-1-78952-052-1

Peter Hammill – Richard Rees Jones 978-1-78952-163-4

Roy Harper – Opher Goodwin 978-1-78952-130-6

Jimi Hendrix – Emma Stott 978-1-78952-175-7

The Hollies – Andrew Darlington 978-1-78952-159-7

Iron Maiden – Steve Pilkington 978-1-78952-061-3

Jefferson Airplane – Richard Butterworth 978-1-78952-143-6

Jethro Tull – Jordan Blum 978-1-78952-016-3

Elton John in the 1970s – Peter Kearns 978-1-78952-034-7

The Incredible String Band – Tim Moon 978-1-78952-107-8

Iron Maiden – Steve Pilkington 978-1-78952-061-3

Judas Priest – John Tucker 978-1-78952-018-7

Kansas – Kevin Cummings 978-1-78952-057-6
The Kinks – Martin Hutchinson 978-1-78952-172-6
Korn – Matt Karpe 978-1-78952-153-5
Led Zeppelin – Steve Pilkington 978-1-78952-151-1
Level 42 – Matt Philips 978-1-78952-102-3
Little Feat – 978-1-78952-168-9
Aimee Mann – Jez Rowden 978-1-78952-036-1
Joni Mitchell – Peter Kearns 978-1-78952-081-1
The Moody Blues – Geoffrey Feakes 978-1-78952-042-2
Motorhead – Duncan Harris 978-1-78952-173-3
Mike Oldfield – Ryan Yard 978-1-78952-060-6
Opeth – Jordan Blum 978-1-78-952-166-5
Tom Petty – Richard James 978-1-78952-128-3
Porcupine Tree – Nick Holmes 978-1-78952-144-3
Queen – Andrew Wild 978-1-78952-003-3
Radiohead – William Allen 978-1-78952-149-8
Renaissance – David Detmer 978-1-78952-062-0
The Rolling Stones 1963-80 – Steve Pilkington 978-1-78952-017-0
The Smiths and Morrissey – Tommy Gunnarsson 978-1-78952-140-5
Status Quo the Frantic Four Years – Richard James 978-1-78952-160-3
Steely Dan – Jez Rowden 978-1-78952-043-9
Steve Hackett – Geoffrey Feakes 978-1-78952-098-9
Thin Lizzy – Graeme Stroud 978-1-78952-064-4
Toto – Jacob Holm-Lupo 978-1-78952-019-4
U2 – Eoghan Lyng 978-1-78952-078-1
UFO – Richard James 978-1-78952-073-6
The Who – Geoffrey Feakes 978-1-78952-076-7
Roy Wood and the Move – James R Turner 978-1-78952-008-8
Van Der Graaf Generator – Dan Coffey 978-1-78952-031-6
Yes – Stephen Lambe 978-1-78952-001-9
Frank Zappa 1966 to 1979 – Eric Benac 978-1-78952-033-0
Warren Zevon – Peter Gallagher 978-1-78952-170-2
10CC – Peter Kearns 978-1-78952-054-5

Decades Series
The Bee Gees in the 1960s – Andrew Môn Hughes et al 978-1-78952-148-1
The Bee Gees in the 1970s – Andrew Môn Hughes et al 978-1-78952-179-5
Black Sabbath in the 1970s – Chris Sutton 978-1-78952-171-9
Britpop – Peter Richard Adams and Matt Pooler 978-1-78952-169-6
Alice Cooper in the 1970s – Chris Sutton 978-1-78952-104-7
Curved Air in the 1970s – Laura Shenton 978-1-78952-069-9
Bob Dylan in the 1980s – Don Klees 978-1-78952-157-3
Fleetwood Mac in the 1970s – Andrew Wild 978-1-78952-105-4
Focus in the 1970s – Stephen Lambe 978-1-78952-079-8

Also available from Sonicbond

Free and Bad Company in the 1970s – John Van der Kiste 978-1-78952-178-8
Genesis in the 1970s – Bill Thomas 978178952-146-7
George Harrison in the 1970s – Eoghan Lyng 978-1-78952-174-0
Marillion in the 1980s – Nathaniel Webb 978-1-78952-065-1
Mott the Hoople and Ian Hunter in the 1970s – John Van der Kiste 978-1-78-952-162-7
Pink Floyd In The 1970s – Georg Purvis 978-1-78952-072-9
Tangerine Dream in the 1970s – Stephen Palmer 978-1-78952-161-0
The Sweet in the 1970s – Darren Johnson from Gary Cosby collection 978-1-78952-139-9
Uriah Heep in the 1970s – Steve Pilkington 978-1-78952-103-0
Yes in the 1980s – Stephen Lambe with David Watkinson 978-1-78952-125-2

On Screen series
Carry On... – Stephen Lambe 978-1-78952-004-0
David Cronenberg – Patrick Chapman 978-1-78952-071-2
Doctor Who: The David Tennant Years – Jamie Hailstone 978-1-78952-066-8
James Bond – Andrew Wild – 978-1-78952-010-1
Monty Python – Steve Pilkington 978-1-78952-047-7
Seinfeld Seasons 1 to 5 – Stephen Lambe 978-1-78952-012-5

Other Books
1967: A Year In Psychedelic Rock – Kevan Furbank 978-1-78952-155-9
1970: A Year In Rock – John Van der Kiste 978-1-78952-147-4
1973: The Golden Year of Progressive Rock 978-1-78952-165-8
Babysitting A Band On The Rocks – G.D. Praetorius 978-1-78952-106-1
Eric Clapton Sessions – Andrew Wild 978-1-78952-177-1
Derek Taylor: For Your Radioactive Children – Andrew Darlington 978-1-78952-038-5
The Golden Road: The Recording History of The Grateful Dead – John Kilbride 978-1-78952-156-6
Iggy and The Stooges On Stage 1967-1974 – Per Nilsen 978-1-78952-101-6
Jon Anderson and the Warriors – the road to Yes – David Watkinson 978-1-78952-059-0
Nu Metal: A Definitive Guide – Matt Karpe 978-1-78952-063-7
Tommy Bolin: In and Out of Deep Purple – Laura Shenton 978-1-78952-070-5
Maximum Darkness – Deke Leonard 978-1-78952-048-4
Maybe I Should've Stayed In Bed – Deke Leonard 978-1-78952-053-8
The Twang Dynasty – Deke Leonard 978-1-78952-049-1

and many more to come!

Would you like to write for Sonicbond Publishing?

At Sonicbond Publishing we are always on the look-out for authors, particularly for our two main series:

On Track. Mixing fact with in depth analysis, the On Track series examines the work of a particular musical artist or group. All genres are considered from easy listening and jazz to 60s soul to 90s pop, via rock and metal.

On Screen. This series looks at the world of film and television. Subjects considered include directors, actors and writers, as well as entire television and film series. As with the On Track series, we balance fact with analysis.

While professional writing experience would, of course, be an advantage the most important qualification is to have real enthusiasm and knowledge of your subject. First-time authors are welcomed, but the ability to write well in English is essential.

Sonicbond Publishing has distribution throughout Europe and North America, and all books are also published in E-book form. Authors will be paid a royalty based on sales of their book.

Further details are available from www.sonicbondpublishing.co.uk. To contact us, complete the contact form there or email info@sonicbondpublishing.co.uk

Follow us on social media:
Twitter: https://twitter.com/SonicbondP
Instagram: https://www.instagram.com/sonicbondpublishing_/
Facebook: https://www.facebook.com/SonicbondPublishing/
Linktree QR code: